SPEAK OF THE DEVILS

DEVILS

THE BOOK OF MANCHESTER UNITED QUOTATIONS

COMPILED BY EUGENE WEBER

WEBER BOOKS.

First published in Great Britain in 1998 by
Weber Books Limited
PO Box 16545
London SE22 8ZR

Printed and bound in Great Britain by Cox & Wyman, Reading, Berkshire.

ISBN 0 9533078 0 8

This is not an official Manchester United publication.

CONTENTS

ACKNOWLEDGEMENTS

I would like to express my gratitude to a great many people and organisations who have helped me to compile this collection.

David Barber, Librarian at the Football Association; Alan Collings of the *Daily Mail*; Warren Wilson, editor of the *Express & Star*; Michael Daly of the *Irish Independent*; Walter McAuley of the *Belfast Telegraph* and Des O'Driscoll of the *Cork Examiner*.

Daniel Norcross, Richard Pigden, Warren Shore, Mike Spear, John Stone and Theo Weber read the manuscript and made invaluable suggestions for improvement.

Donna Blackburn, Eugene Wolstenholme and Simon Skelly helped me wrestle with the complexities of Quark Express. However, Don Wright saved the day when all appeared lost.

I would also like to thank the following: Mark Baxter, Mark Brock, Stuart Dempster, Brian Farmer, Bob Foster, David Goddard, Martin Liu, Moira Whittle and Aine, Alexander and Leander Wolstenholme.

INTRODUCTION

I became a Manchester United supporter as a nine-year-old in Dublin when my brother, who lived in Manchester at the time and was on a visit home, claimed he played for United. I obviously displayed a healthly scepticism because he went off and returned a few minutes later with a pair of green and white socks to prove his point. I was convinced and became a United supporter there and then.

Luckily, there was no lasting psychological damage inflicted on such a young mind from this subterfuge. I could have rebelled, turned delinquent and become a Manchester City supporter.

When I discovered the truth about my brother and the socks, I took it all in my stride.

But it did begin a lifelong interest in United. I can remember my brother giving me graphic accounts of the Munich disaster, of ordinary people weeping in the streets and the sense of catastrophe weighing on the city of Manchester.

Every time United came to Dublin to play exhibition matches, huge crowds would turn out to see them. The atmosphere would be celebratory. I saw Best, Law and Charlton on a number of occasions. The crowd would be hoping Best would beat eight men before scoring and hoping Bobby Charlton would burst the net with a pile driver from 40 yards. We would always want United to win and the local team to lose, whereas we always supported the local team when other clubs visited from England.

Later, I moved to London and when I was working at the Press Association we decided to form a football team. I was the only person to own a football - a QPR one at that. Our first practice session took place in Green Park, but we were told to leave by a warden - it being a Royal park, football was forbidden. We retreated to a nearby pub in Piccadilly and who should walk in with a tall blonde but George Best. Being the bashful type I managed to persuade one of my colleagues to go and ask him to sign the ball. Best signed and was happy to do so. I must be the only person to have a QPR ball signed by the great man.

When the idea to compile the book first occurred to me I was sure it must have been done before. I was amazed to discover it hadn't and set about researching straight away.

And what a joy it was to spend hours and hours and months and months poring over material, from the earliest days to the present. One thing I've leaned for certain is that United never wore green and white socks!

I hope you get as much pleasure reading this book as I did compiling it.

Eugene Weber, London 1998.

SIR MATT

If Busby had stood dressed for the pit, and somebody alongside him in the room had worn ermine, there would have been no difficulty about deciding who was special. Granting him a knighthood did not elevate him. It raised, however briefly, the whole dubious phenomenon of the honours system.

HUGH McILVANNEY, journalist.

Busby emanated presence, substance, the quality of strength without arrogance. No man in my experience ever exemplified better the ability to treat you as an equal while leaving you with the sure knowledge that you were less than he was. Such men do not have to be appointed leaders. Some democracy of the instincts and the blood elects them to be in charge.

HUGH McILVANNEY.

Matt Busby is a symbol of everything that is best in our national game.

HAROLD WILSON.

He is flawless in his dealing with us. He can remain aloof and yet human. He can tear us apart and still command respect. He can praise us, and we know it to be genuine. He can advise us and we know there is no dark motive afoot. He can talk to us and we will always listen. The manager-player relationship at Old Trafford is ideal.

GEORGE BEST.

I have often been asked what made Matt Busby so special and really it was the simplest thing in the world. He treated his players like human beings !

DENIS LAW.

I give you the answer in three words: skill, fitness and character; and the greatest of these is character.

MATT BUSBY on the key attributes of a United player.

In a way Matt is like a successful preacher. He makes you believe what he believes. His way of doing things the only way of doing things. His mixture of personal humility and ruthless judgement is what makes the challenge of being a Manchester United player so exhilarating. You know you won't be judged by match results, but individually by mysterious standards buried deep inside Matt himself and only him.

ALBERT QUIXALL, who played in the late 1950s and early 1960s.

A footballer has come into this house today.

THE DOCTOR at Matt Busby's birth.

There have been some great managers in this country like Herbert Chapman, Bill Nicholson and Bill Shankly, but without doubt he's the greatest there has been.

ALEX FERGUSON paying tribute to Matt Busby when he died.

They should rename Old Trafford the Matt Busby Stadium because for so many years he was Manchester United.

TOMMY DOCHERTY.

Football has probably lost the greatest ambassador it has ever known. No matter what era he had been manager, he would have been the greatest.

DENIS LAW.

I think he put Manchester on the map more than any other human being, not just United but Manchester itself.

PAT CRERAND.

Let the angels help him make a team that will give divine pleasure to all the souls in Heaven, just as his boys gave joy here on earth

HAROLD RILEY, painter, at Matt Busby's funeral.

I remember my father telling me as a young boy that you don't meet more than three great people in you life. I know I met one.

ALEX FERGUSON.

Sir Matt Busby's gift for leadership owed much to his mystique, the elusive force men imagined lay behind the facade of genial composure. Old players, even the greatest of them, who shared extraordinary days and nights with Busby, remain in awe of him. They speak of always wanting to please him. Long after they were famous, universally adored and in all worldly ways secure, it was Sir Matt's attention and affection men like Bobby Charlton,Johnny Carey, Denis Law, George Best and Harry Gregg craved. Great athletes felt inadequate in his presence, although he had ostensibly done nothing to induce the feeling.

EAMON DUNPHY, journalist and former United player.

Unwittingly, Matt was football's first public relations officer. He was a manager alright, but also a brilliant PRO. He was a hand-shaker and kisser of babies. A club would pay him millions to do that job today.

HARRY GREGG.

Some people called me a visionary, others a reactionary, while a few called me awkward or stubborn.

MATT BUSBY on the club's foray into Europe despite the disapproval of the Football League.

Prestige alone demanded that the Continental challenge should be met, not avoided.

MATT BUSBY.

I have never met anyone else like him in the game. The longer you knew him the more you felt for him, which was why he had everybody doing the things they did.

DENIS LAW.

Footballers are people first, that was Busby's secret. Even the oldest men were boys to him.

EAMON DUNPHY.

He was the outstanding man of them all - even Bill Shankly and Jock Stein sought his advice and experience.

ALEX FERGUSON.

You could easily be fooled into accepting Busby as everyone's kind uncle. That's how he comes over to the public. But he can be as practical and cunning as the best of them. As far as I am concerned he has been the greatest manager of his time and at times one of the toughest.

MAURICE SETTERS, who played in the early 1960s.

In a business often petty and peevish, often unbalanced with it's brush-stroke speed from success to failure, he has long since won regard and respect. Won them in the fullest measure without once courting them.

Football Monthly on Matt Busby.

Every manager should have a hobby. Mine is soccer.

MATT BUSBY.

SIR MATT

Matt was one of the most entertaining and cultured players of his day. He has proved himself to be the most outstanding manager of his time. But to those of us who knew him intimately, the most striking characteristic about the man is that one could not wish to meet a nicer fellow.

CLIFF BRITTON, manager and player.

Quite simply Matt is a good fellow. A person of whom one is very pleased to be able to say: 'yes, I knew him well'. A man who has achieved greatness on and off the field with his good head and kind heart.

ARTHUR ROWE, former Spurs manager.

Matt Busby is without a shadow of a doubt, I suppose, Mr. Football. He is the first person most fans think of when they think of football managers. And as far as players are concerned, well, he's a kind of idol.

NOEL CANTWELL.

Some of us are happy to produce one good side - Matt has pro-duced four and perhaps there is a fifth one coming through. Matt is certainly the best manager of good players I know. A player stands or falls in his eyes on his ability alone. Other things aren't so important. He can charm people into playing or even thinking his way. But when the occasion warrants it he can be ruthless in the interests of Manchester United.

JOE MERCER.

Legend is the most over-used word in football today, but if we can't use it about Sir Matt Busby to whom can we apply it?

JOYCE WOOLRIDGE, journalist.

The figurehead of all figureheads - he is Manchester United.

RAY WILKINS on Matt Busby

Matt will seek the board's advice, ponder over it and then go away and do precisely as he wants.

HAROLD HARDMAN, former chairman of United

Matt Busby is without doubt the greatest manager that ever lived. I'm not saying that I think he's the greatest manager, I'm saying he is the greatest manager.

BILL SHANKLY.

No one tells me who to put into my team and who to drop.

MATT BUSBY to Liam Whelan who asked to be dropped.

Everything that's been said about Matt since he died was said before he died. That's the greatest epitaph that he could have.

WILLIE MORGAN.

Matt was still struggling to recover from the injuries he received at Munich. He walked with a stick. Jimmy Murphy walked alongside, lending him a hand. In complete silence, Matt walked round our dressing room, shaking every player by the hand. He congratulated us all individually. Something - something very special - made that man come into our dressing room in what must have been one of the saddest moments of his life to congratulate us on beating his team. Tommy Banks summed it up for us all when he said: 'That's the finest sportsman you'll ever see.' No wonder Matt's teams always played for him. How could you fail respect a man like that.

NAT LOFTHOUSE on Matt Busby after the 1958 F.A Cup final , a few months after the Munich tragedy.

He managed with a velvet glove. A kind man, a generous man, beautiful man. But everyone at Old Trafford knew who was the manager.

BOBBY ROBSON.

So many of the good things in life have come my way since I became a professional footballer, it sometimes does me good to think back on the day when living was not so easy. It helps me keep my feet on the ground.

MATT BUSBY.

Big talk in the dressing room was one thing, dealing with 'The Boss' in his office was a very different experience. His presence was overwhelming. You were not confronted, on the contrary, he was charming, solicitous, understanding your concerns, keen that you should understand Manchester United's interests as well as your own. He didn't make you feel bad, he made you feel important, you wanted to please him, do what was right for everyone, yourself and the club. He was the club. You signed. And felt like a shit for causing hassle in the first place. Then you thanked him. On the way down the stairs you tried to figure out a way to explain to the others what had happened.

EAMON DUNPHY on Matt Busby.

Today's a sad day. I never met him but I saw him thousands of times. He loved everyone - he must have done to put up with George Best.

DOREEN CATTERALL, a United supporter at Matt Busby's funeral.

Manchester United 0, Heaven 1.

BANNER at Matt Busby' funeral.

You wouldn't be playing for me if you were not the best. And we thought: ' He thinks that much of me - how can I let him down. '

PAT CRERAND on Matt Busby.

TRAGEDY

At first I thought I was the only one left. I could not realise I was alive myself. In fact I thought I was dreaming.

HARRY GREGG after the Munich air crash.

Yesterday on Munich airfield, Association football shrank to a small matter.

THE GUARDIAN newspaper.

A man in dungarees - which on the Old Trafford terraces is a kind of supporter's uniform- came into the public bar and said: ' I still can't credit it. ' He pulled a bundle of programme vouchers out of his pocket - representing all the season's games he had seen - and threw them down irritably: ' There, best team in the blinkin' world'.

A UNITED SUPPORTER after the Munich air disaster.

Even if it means being heavily defeated we will carry on with the season's programme. We have a duty to the public.

HAROLD HARDMAN, the Manchester United Chairman, after the Munich air crash.

The moment Manchester United took the field the plainsong rose from the ground. One has heard a roar on many fields and in many parts but never one like that. In it there was a proud defiance, turning away any sympathy or mercy and from that moment life was blown into the embers of the night.

THE TIMES newspaper on United's first game after the Munich disaster

TRAGEDY

Before the start the crowd of 60,000 stood in silence for a minute in memory of those who died in Munich. This solemnity dissolved in a roar of welcome when the United team, led by Foulkes, the new captain, ran onto the field. Foulkes and Gregg, the goalkeeper, two survivors of the crash, were warmly cheered for almost everything they did throughout the game. It seemed gallant of them to be there at all and much more than that to play as spiritedly as they did. With the cheers of welcome was mingled a kind of sigh, as though a weight had been lifted cheers. They will almost have heard them in Munich.

THE GUARDIAN newspaper on the same game.

The United, fashioned by Mr. Busby became a work of art. That has now been slashed tragically and the loss to British football may be deep.

THE TIMES newspaper.

Whenever, some time in the future, soccer old timers are trying to remember what that Manchester United side was really like, one eager chunky figure will tend to come pounding into their minds. Duncan Edwards, perhaps more than any of his team mates, represented the spirit of the side.
Watching him, you always felt that he would be glad to join in a scratch game between coats in the local park and would play there with the same unflagging concentration and exuberance that he put into a floodlit European Cup game. The whole team was rather like that but this young buccaneer most of all and it put him deeply under the skin of the Old Trafford crowd.

AN OBITUARY for Duncan Edwards.

We have the greatest sympathy with Manchester United, but if industry let everyone walk out to watch a funeral, things would just stop.

VINCENT HARNEY, Production Manager of Boxmakers Manchester, defending the sacking of 22 female staff for attending the funeral of Eddie Colman.

Their return to Old Trafford was a poignant night. Girls wearing scarves with pictures of the dead players edged in black wept. As United scored the first of their three goals a man near the Press box looked up into the shadows outside the floodlights and said: 'One of them helped it in. '

ROLAND ALLEN, journalist.

At six o'clock out of pure curiosity, I turned on my television set. As the news came on the screen seemed to go black. The normally urbane voice of the announcer seemed to turn into a sledge-hammer. I sat listening with a frozen brain to that cruel and shocking list of casualties that was now to give to the word Munich an even sadder meaning than it had acquired on a day before the war when a British Prime Minister had come home to London waving a pitiful piece of paper and most of us knew that new calamities of war were inevitable.

H.E.. BATES, writer.

Sheffield Wednesday had no chance, and I felt sorry for them. I don't think they had any heart for the fight. The crowd was hysterical and I was not far off being the same way.

BILL FOULKES on United's first match after the Munich disaster.

I was lost and sorrowing, and for a short period utterly defeated. A man's help at such a time is not his experience, but his faith and the love and encouragement of his friends.

MATT BUSBY.

I wasn't hurt. I wasn't even deeply troubled in mind. I just couldn't take it in, and therefore it washed over me. I didn't want to accept what happened.

BOBBY CHARLTON.

Sometimes I still see them play.

MATT BUSBY.

It would have been as pointless for me to ask the pilot if everything was okay as if he had asked me whether I had picked the best team for Manchester United.

MATT BUSBY replying when asked why he had not refused to travel on the plane back from Munich.

I was at my lowest ebb since the Munich air crash and it was in my mind to turn my back on football altogether. It seemed the fates had conspired against the club and myself.

MATT BUSBY after being knocked out of the European Cup by Partizan Belgrade in 1967.

The moment when Bobby took the Cup it cleansed me. It eased the pain of the guilt of going into Europe. It was my justification.

MATT BUSBY after winning the European Cup in 1968.

The surgeons felt he might live but no one except those close to him ever felt he would be a force again in football. But I knew. In one of his conscious moments he waved a feeble hand for me to come to his side. I had to bend low over his bed to catch his words: 'keep the flag flying, Jimmy. Keep things going until I get back. '

JIMMY MURPHY on Matt Busby.

I know it sounds terrible but my career must have been helped by that tragedy. I mean, how could I have displaced anyone like Eddie Colman. He was genius.

NOBBY STILES.

To start with I was in complete turmoil through sheer sorrow. I also felt completely on my own. Not only was Matt not there, but my great friend, Bert Whalley our coach, had been killed and so had Tom Curry, the trainer.

JIMMY MURPHY.

February 19, 1958. The silent minute when 59,848 people at Old Trafford, Manchester, mourned the footballers who had been killed on the Munich Airport 13 days earlier, seemed more like a year. It was almost possible to hear their tears drop.

ALAN HOVE, journalist.

Before it happened I could see ten years ahead, ten years at the top. After it, I had two choices, either to lie down and hide, or pick up the challenge. My wife Jean and the people of Manchester made the decision for me.

MATT BUSBY.

At first I felt I was going out of my mind, not knowing where to start.

JIMMY MURPHY in the immediate aftermath of the Munich disaster when he had to run the club.

I'll never forget it. I came home right away and confirmed it. I didn't know what to think, I was numb. I had sent Liam Whelan over there and the hardest thing I ever had to do was to go over to Cabra and meet his mother. I knew he was dead, but I wasn't sure whether she knew or not. When I went over it was terrible. They were a lovely family.

BILLY BEHAN, United's Ireland scout after the Munich disaster.

Matt was at death's door but when he started to get well I went over to see him to tell him I was retiring, told him I couldn't face sending a player away any more. But he said: 'Well, how do you think I feel ?' And I said: 'It's like this Matt, you're the strand, I'm only a grain of sand on the strand, don't start comparing me with you.' But he said: 'We think you're more than that.' So I said I would stay as long as he stayed.

BILLY BEHAN.

If the worst happens, I am ready for death. I hope we all are.

LIAM WHELAN'S last words.

Thank God he is safe. He has always been a good son and I knew he would come to no harm.

JACKIE BLANCHFLOWER'S MUM.

My wife Jean says I'm bitter, but I don't think so really. I became depressed and did nothing for a couple of years. It was not that I couldn't do anything. I just did not want to do anything.

JACKIE BLANCHFLOWER after retiring because of injuries sustained in the Munich disaster.

The kids who follow United now are fanatics, but I believe that fanaticism stemmed from that day in Munich. A team died but I believe a club was born.

ALBERT SCANLON.

I am a Catholic. I have always believed in the after-life, but what was an after-life to those lads? What power was it that could allow them to be destroyed? It had shaken my faith. I was very mixed up in the mind. I was absolutely certain that I would have no more to do with football. I didn't want to see anyone who had the remotest connection with the game. I was horrible to live with.

MATT BUSBY.

The word 'great' is used too lightly these days. You only have to turn on the television to see a 'great' pass, pick up a paper to read about a 'great' game, switch on the radio to hear about a 'great' goal. They can't all be great. But the Busby Babes were great. Great players, a great team, great people. Great days. Their death stunned the world. Not just Manchester, not just Lancashire, not just Britain. The world.

NAT LOFTHOUSE.

Is the kick-off at 3 o'clock, Jimmy ?

DUNCAN EDWARDS to Jimmy Murphy as he was lying in hospital.

I doubt whether Real Madrid would have won as much as they did if that United side had survived.

BOBBY CHARLTON.

I always felt as if we were cheating somehow. Stepping into other people's shoes. I felt in a way I shouldn't have been there.

IAN GREAVES who came into the United team after Munich.

I often think about that time and the team we had in the 1950s. And I love talking about it, because it gives me pleasure not sadness.

WILF McGUINNESS.

I want the best team in the country again - and I'll have it.

MATT BUSBY to Dennis Viollet.

It's so tragic. Duncan hung on so long. I think we all thought he was going to live.

ARTHUR OAKLEY, Director of Wolverhamptom Wanderers.

A truly amazing boy who, apart from being a great footballer, devoted his life to sport and supported all manners of good living.

MATT BUSBY on Duncan Edwards at the unveiling of a memorial window to him in St. Francis' Church in Dudley.

He fought with all the unforgettable fury of that unconquerable spirit. And when he died a great sigh went round the sports fields. It was though a young Colossus had been taken from our midst.

FRANK TAYLOR, journalist, on Duncan Edwards.

THE BEAUTIFUL GAME

Gazza said recently that scoring a goal was better than an orgasm. Lee Chapman said it wasn't as good. I think I'll go with Pele - he thought it was about the same.

RYAN GIGGS.

When things go wrong for us there always seem to be critics who like to dwell on the fact that I once said that our forwards are given free expression......we are as alive to the need for tactics as any other team; and I submit that no team can achieve our measure of success over the years without some sort of method. But I mean what I say about freedom of expression, too For when a team has international players like Denis Law, Bobby Charlton and George Best in attack they have their own ideas and it is a waste of talent to subject them to a list of do's and don'ts.

MATT BUSBY.

Benfica were more than just beaten, they were pulverised.

THE SUN newspaper after United's stunning 5-1 win over Benfica in the European Cup in 1967.

This was our finest hour.

MATT BUSBY after the same match..

I imagine the ball to be alive, sensitive, responding to the touch of my foot, to my caresses, like a woman with the man she loves.

ERIC CANTONA.

I was surprised by Manchester United. Here, at Old Trafford they are actually keeping the ball on the turf in attack, instead of thumping it all over the premises and are running into position to receive passes.

A SUNDAY CHRONICLE newspaper report after United beat Chelsea 5-1 in 1938.

Of course I wasn't nervous. Taking a penalty to win the Cup is what you are in the game for. If you don't feel excited by that, perhaps you should not be a professional footballer.

ERIC CANTONA who scored two penalties in the 1994 F.A. Cup final.

Every day I wake up and if there's a football game to play or watch it is like Christmas Day to me.

BOBBY CHARLTON..

I never wanted Manchester United to be second to anybody. Only the best would be good enough. I had to have players who would play for me and for United rather than for themselves, if you understand what I mean. And I usually found what I wanted.

MATT BUSBY.

I love taking the piss out of players too. Like 'nutmegging' them. That's sticking it between their legs and running round them. When I first started I did not mind the hard men too much because it gave me the chance to rubbish them with my skill. I'd go past them and they'd say: 'Do that again and I'll break your f****** leg!' And next time I'd do them again and they'd say: 'Right, I f****** warned you'. Next time I got the ball I'd stand on it and beckon them to me. I used to be like a bullfighter, inviting them to charge me. They rarely got me. I was too quick. At moments like that, with the crowd cheering I used to get the horn. Honestly. it used to arouse me, excite me.

GEORGE BEST.

Shellito was taken off suffering from twisted blood.

PAT CRERAND after Chelsea's full back Ken Shellito was run ragged by George Best.

Beyond my wildest dreams.

ALEX FERGUSON after United beat FC Porto 4-0 at Old Trafford in the Champion's' League in 1997.

In the modern game of football there are great musicians, but Glenn Hoddle is like Mozart among the hard rock men.

ERIC CANTONA.

A good goal is one which is important and beautiful.

ERIC CANTONA.

The Soviet Union had opened up to the outside world under the twin themes of glasnost and perestroika. United's Ukrainian capture chimed very much in the spirit of the times. It was not long before Kanchelskis himself was opening up defences and restructuring a few luckless full-backs in the time-honoured fashion of flying Manchester United wingers.

PATRICK TOOHER, writer.

They were the best days of my life. We used to just go out and attack teams. If somebody scored three against us we knew we'd get four. It was great just going out on the pitch. We knew we'd enjoy it.

STUART PEARSON.

I never subscribed to Sir Alf Ramsey's doctrine of hard running off the ball. I am a footballer - and that means having a football at my feet.

GEORGE BEST.

I remember one game where Best glided past Harris' waist high tackle, struck the ball through Marvin Hinton's legs, sent Eddie McCreadie one way and Bonetti the other before scoring. If he'd only gone past nightclubs the way he did defenders, he'd still be playing.

WILF McGUINNESS, who succeeded Matt Busby as manager.

All the best players have imagination, they see a bigger picture. I watch a game and they will play a pass and I will think: 'Bloody hell, I never saw that ' That is what a great player can do. We try to develop that here, we ask them: ' What have you got in your locker? Show us what you can do? '

ALEX FERGUSON.

When you see Ryan Giggs play football it is as though an enchanted sprite is dancing on the still surface of a golden pond. Then the referee blows his whistle and the sprite is gone. This is partly by design, partly by circumstance. Practically, his Manchester United employers cannot put him in a glass case and lock him away between matches. But they would if they could.

JAMES LAWTON, journalist.

What times. What matches they were. United were always the benchmark for us, glamorous, sophisticated, packed with stars. George Best, Bobby Charlton and Denis Law. We were the pretenders, they were the kings. And we told them we wanted their crown. In those days we were an uncouth lot and tested the laws to the limits.

BILLY BREMNER, the former Leeds United captain.

I scored my first big-time goal and what a feeling I got - something I can never hope to describe. It seemed I would burst with happiness.

LIAM WHELAN.

THE BEAUTIFUL GAME

A quick goal is one way to counter the defence-minded sides, as they have got to come out to fight back. But in exaggerated 'blanket ' games such as seen in Italy, and too often in Britain these days, there is little chance for forwards. But there is a big chance that the game will be ruined as a spectacle if it is sacrificed on the altar of cold science.

MATT BUSBY.

When he waggled his hips he made the stanchions in the grandstand sway.

HARRY GREGG on Eddie 'snake hips' Colman.

Football is still the greatest game in the world. The trouble is that the fun seems to have gone from it, and we shall have to put it back. I would say far more emphatically today than I would have said when I was a younger player, and there was some fun in it: Yes, do put your son on the football stage Mr.Worthington if he seems to have what it takes. Because, for all its tensions, football is one of the healthiest professions and among the best paid for the most successful.

MATT BUSBY.

Football is not about profit and loss. It is about glory and excitement, about loyalty and legends, about local identity and family history, about skills and talents, none of which can be computed on balance sheets. Football doesn't have a product. Every year United fans have their ashes scattered on the turf at Old Trafford. How often do you see that happening at Tesco?

HUNTER DAVIES, writer and journalist.

It's always been adventure and romance for United.

PAT CRERAND.

You can watch a replay of his magic and still you cannot see how it was possible.

DAVID COLEMAN on George Best.

That goal changed me - not as a person, but as a player. People have looked at me differently ever since.

DAVID BECKHAM on the goal he scored from the halfway line against Wimbledon in the first match of the 1996-97 season.

It's one of those goals that I will look back on in a few years time and think, 'did I really do that ?'

DAVID BECKHAM on the same wonder goal.

I went up to David afterwards, shook his hand and called him a bastard and we had a little laugh about it.

NEIL SULLIVAN, the Wimbledon goalkeeper who was beaten by Beckham's shot

They can keep showing that goal on television. Who knows it might get me a fast-food advertising contract. I like pizza.

NEIL SULLIVAN

The bewildering repertoire of feints and swerves, sudden stops and demoralising spurts, exploited a freakish elasticity of limb and torso, tremendous physical strength and balance that would have made Isaac Newton decide he might as well have eaten the apple.

HUGH McILVANNEY, journalist, on George Best.

There is nothing finer than seeing him flying down the wing like a gazelle, leaving players in his wake.

MARTIN EDWARDS, United Chief Executive, on Ryan Giggs.

Why don't they pick the whole side for England? The best teams from Hungary have never beaten us like this.

JEF MERMANS of Anderlecht after a 10-0 defeat by United in the European Cup in 1956.

THE BEAUTIFUL GAME

An artist, in my eyes, is someone who can lighten up a dark room. I have never, and never will, find any difference between the pass from Pele to Carlos Alberto in the final of the World Cup in 1970 and the poetry of the young Rimbaud. There is, in each of these human manifestations, an expression of beauty which touches us and gives us a feeling of eternity.

ERIC CANTONA.

Thank you for letting me play your beautiful football.

ERIC CANTONA accepting his award as PFA Player of the Year.

He's more than just a circus act with his flicks and back heels....Cantona has a picture of what's going on all around him, wide vision. He can see round corners.

WILF McGUINNESS.

Never mind the fact that he has exquisite touch and incredible vision, Cantona is simply something else - sort of mystical in a way. And I've felt the hairs on the back of my neck stand up just watching him training

ANDY COLE.

He [Rimbaud] was the pioneer, but the torch he lit was picked up by others like Jim Morrison and I believe that, even in football, I should live as instinctively as that.

ERIC CANTONA.

He has not been staled by knocks or mud or the dragging weight of repetition. He does not make a crowd think murder; what he gives them is delight.

ARTHUR HOPCRAFT, journalist, on Bobby Charlton.

Cruyff was manufactured on Earth. George Best was made in Heaven.

DEREK DOUGAN, the former Wolves and Northern Ireland player.

Bobby Charlton - the dashing leader of the line on a white charger, releasing rockets from the edge of the area that go home like a clap of thunder and lift the opposing net as if a gale had struck it.

GEOFFREY GREEN, journalist.

He is arguably the best foreign ambassador this country has had among common people. He has epitomised the sportsmanship and integrity which was once taken for granted in the British character, and has maintained his unblemished record of never being cautioned, in spite of all the provocation, through a period when the game has been increasingly nasty.

DAVID MILLER, journalist, on Bobby Charlton.

When I'm on the field nothing gives me more pleasure than making a fool of somebody.

GEORGE BEST.

George Best can do more things than anyone in all history. He is a magnificent distributor of the ball. He can beat a man on either side using methods that no one has ever before thought about, he can shoot, head, tackle and keep cooler than anyone at the same time.

PAT CRERAND.

That game in Portugal for me was something of a starting point. That was probably the occasion when I decided it was only going to get better. From that match on I actually believed there was nobody better than me. It is amazing what one performance can do.

GEORGE BEST recalling United's 5-1 defeat of Benfica in Portugal in the European Cup 1966..

George [Best] knows he let a lot of people down a lot of times. But what he also did was to make people's dreams come true.

DENIS LAW.

THE BEAUTIFUL GAME

Sir Stanley Matthews should be looking over his shoulder. His reputation as the finest entertainer in British soccer is in danger of being overhauled. By, of course, George Best of Manchester United.

TOM FINNEY.

Let him alone. Don't try and coach him. The boy is special.

MATT BUSBY'S advice to the training staff at Old Trafford after George Best arrived.

He had ice in his veins, warmth in his heart and timing and balance in his feet.

DANNY BLANCHFLOWER on George Best.

The fundamentals of the game are the same today as they were in my playing days; it is my aim to make footballers out of my boys, and if I succeed, the tactics are comparatively easy to solve.

MATT BUSBY.

Perhaps it is simply because I have got older, but the soccer scene today doesn't excite me as much as when I made my debut eight years ago. Everything was new and exciting. I believe that my job is to entertain the people who have paid money to see me play. One of the big problems with modern-day soccer is that it has become too stereotyped with everybody preoccupied with defence.

GEORGE BEST in 1972.

Ryan [Giggs] can actually do things I just remember doing.

BOBBY CHARLTON.

We can be patient if we have to, but in the end it's our nature to try to tear the other lot to pieces.

TOMMY DOCHERTY.

SPEAK OF THE DEVILS

It was Christmas Day every Saturday.

PAT CRERAND.

If you are going to be beaten, you don't mind if it's by the great man himself.

GEORGE BEST after he came second to Pele in a worldwide poll to see who was the greatest-ever player on the planet.

United have grown so much in stature, even in the course of this season, that they look like supermen. Butt and Berg, in particular, were kicked from pillar to post yesterday, but, just like some foot-balling version of Arnold Schwarzenegger in *The Terminator* , they kept getting up when everyone was sure they would have to stay down. To Blackburn, United are taking on a collective aura of an indestructible machine.

OLIVER HOLT, journalist, reporting on United's 4-0 win over Blackburn Rovers in November 1997.

I'd give all the champagne I've ever drunk to be playing along side him in a big European match at Old Trafford.

GEORGE BEST on Eric Cantona.

When I put the ball in the net I didn't know what to do, didn't know how to celebrate. I didn't know so I just ran. I bet I looked a fool on television.

PHIL NEVILLE, after scoring his first goal for United against Chelsea.

Let me say, here and now, that I do not believe in tactics. There is a lot of rot talked by a lot of people about tactics and coaching. These are the people who wear their lapel badges to boost their ego, take their holidays at Lilleshall and talk of the coaching man-ual as if it was a football bible.

GEORGE BEST.

COMING & GOING

One minute we're thinking: he's an ugly, French, one eye-browed git, then he crosses the Pennines and becomes a dark, brooding, Heathcliff-type.

A FAN after United signed Cantona.

There's got to be some common sense about the transfer market. At £3.6 million and the personal terms you're right up against it.

ALEX FERGUSON explaining why he didn't sign Alan Shearer.

Every signing you make is a gamble. But look at Andy's goal record. Some people would pay £10 million for that.

ALEX FERGUSON after signing Andy Cole for £7 million.

When he was playing in Russia he was earning £2 a month. Last year we paid him £350,000. What does he want?

ALEX FERGUSON after Andrei Kanchelskis' request for a transfer.

It was the day Stalin died. But, for Manchester United fans, the more important news was the signing of the Barnsley centre-forward, Tommy Taylor.

STEPHEN F KELLY, writer.

I just don't understand him. But perhaps the problem is that he can't understand the questions of the Scottish reporters.

ALEX FERGUSON on reports that Andrei Kanchelskis wanted to join Glasgow Rangers.

My heart is with United but I can't stay for one reason, and that's the manager.

ANDREI KANCHELSKIS.

Old Trafford, win or lose, is a place you hate leaving. The ground and Manchester United are like a disease - once into your bloodstream there is no escaping their charm and passion for good football.

BRYAN ROBSON.

Every signing you make is a gamble - even if it's for five bob.

ALEX FERGUSON.

It's a vital stage in my career. If I was just going to be sitting on the bench or part of the squad I would stagnate a little bit. The animal in me says I have got to play on.

STEVE BRUCE explaining why he left United to join Birmingham City.

I'd been over there since leaving school and it was a sad day when I had to pack my bags.

DAVID McCREERY.

Sell Bobby Charlton? I would as soon sell myself.

MATT BUSBY.

In the past few days I have signed up for more money than I've earned in all the 14 years as a footballer.

CHARLIE MITTEN after signing for the Santa Fe club of Colombia in 1950
.

When I asked about Eric's availability I wasn't worrying about his temperament. I was trying to bring a huge talent to Old Trafford.

ALEX FERGUSON.

When I signed him from Shrewsbury for £100,000, Harry Gregg said: 'You've got a player who doesn't know the meaning of defeat.' A week later I phoned Harry back and said: 'Aye, and defeat's not the only word he doesn't know the meaning of. There's passing, control, dribble....'

TOMMY DOCHERTY on Jim Holton.

He has found his spiritual home.

ALEX FERGUSON on Eric Cantona in 1993.

We're just very grateful he's here. He's such a great player. I'm still pinching myself. A player like that only comes along once or twice in a lifetime, and you don't leave him out or put him in the reserves. You respect his skill. Eric is the brainiest player I've seen, he sees such a lot when he is on the ball and this team is perfectly suited to him.

BOBBY CHARLTON on Eric Cantona.

Mon plaisir, Eric Cantona.

ALEX FERGUSON introducing Eric Cantona to the world's press.

He's the player to light up our stadium.

ALEX FERGUSON after signing Eric Cantona.

I think I was a long way down the manager's pecking order. There was a lot of talk of Terry Butcher and others, there were a lot of central defenders around at the time. I think the manager just went down the list and eventually stumbled across my name.

STEVE BRUCE.

I'm definitely not interested.

MALCOLM ALLISON, then Manchester City boss, after George Best was put on the transfer list.

It's a tragedy so much talent is going unharnessed.

RON SAUNDERS, then Norwich City manager, on the same event.

He loves wheeling and dealing, but he's not in the Ron Atkinson mould, with a chequebook as big as his ego. He's always looking for a bargain - an uncut diamond he can polish.

JIM WHITE, journalist, on Alex Ferguson.

Let's be honest, Alan Shearer knew he would have been a little fish in a big pond at Old Trafford.

A UNITED Fan after Alan Shearer signed for Newcastle United.

Ex Manchester United players are meant to have wings on their feet or something.

FRANCIS BURNS, United full-back in the late 1960s and early 1970s

I don't sign centre halves with earrings.

RON ATKINSON to Paul McGrath.

Half a million for Remi Moses? You could get the original Moses and the tablets for that price.

TOMMY DOCHERTY.

It's the kind of problem I wouldn't like to inherit, let alone buy.

JOE MERCER, then Coventry boss, on Best's transfer.

He's like Steve Coppell with tricks.

RON ATKINSON after signing Jesper Olsen.

After ten years at Luton, they are the only club in the world I would have left for in my testimonial year.

MAL DONAGHY.

I regret the day I left United. I must have been a fool. They are a truly great club. The players were marvellous to me and the fans treated me and my family with love and respect.

ANDREI KANCHELSKIS.

It would, perhaps, be important for United, for me to come back, but I have no desire.

ERIC CANTONA.

Alex [Ferguson] and I parted on an amicable basis. The media were definitely wrong on that score. The tabloids offered me £50,000 to slag him off and I didn't do it.

NORMAN WHITESIDE.

It's a drag for me to leave. I love the club and have been here since I was 15.

RUSSELL BEARDSMORE.

I just want to go to the World Cup with a Manchester United shirt and contract in my bag.

JAAP STAM.

I leave when I need to change. It's like being with a woman. If you get to the point when you've got nothing left to say to her, you leave. Or else you stop being good.

ERIC CANTONA.

DECLINE

They'd done it, they were proud and they had every reason to be. And then they sat back and you could almost hear the energy and ambition sighing out of the club. It was not that the willingness to win had disappeared completely. It was still there. But after the European Cup it didn't seem quite so important. It was like being in at the winding up of a company.

GEORGE BEST.

It was the worst Manchester United side I have played against in ten years. There was no method about the team and they rarely came out of defence, with even striker Brian Kidd playing back on the edge of his own penalty area. United have enthusiasm, but it is not to win. Just to avoid being beaten and I feel sorry for them in many way because they have to live up to the old United tradition.

TOMMY SMITH, the Liverpool defender, in 1973

Words cannot describe how sick I feel at this moment. I can't believe this has happened, but I know it has.

TOMMY DOCHERTY after United were relegated.

I blame myself partly because I brought a lot of the players to the club and recently we have not had as much success with youngsters.

JOE ARMSTRONG, scout, on the same event.

Teams used to have three men marking George. In the end they didn't bother to stick a man on him.

MALCOLM MUSGROVE, Frank O'Farrell's assistant.

It was disappointing to go down but towards the end of the season a pattern of play began to emerge again and this gives us confidence for the future.

MATT BUSBY.

While I was there the foundations of a once great club were eaten away by internal squabbling. Team spirit vanished and players went into revolt. The club was rife with petty jealousies, an unfriendly, almost hostile place to be. There were players who hardly bothered to talk to me or acknowledge that I was around the place. Bobby Charlton and George Best for instance, they were great performers, but I lost respect for them. They would not talk to each other off the park and during the game seldom passed to each other.

TED MacDOUGALL.

They are one or two players short and some of those they've got need a good talking to.

BOB PAISLEY on United in the early '80s.

In all my 40 years as a player, manager and director, I've never been in the second division. It's a terrible disappointment.

MATT BUSBY.

Being wise after the event, I would say that relegation was a blessing in disguise.

MATT BUSBY.

FANS

At Liverpool, fans asked for Ryan Gigg's and Lee Sharpe's autographs. When they got them they ripped them up in front of their faces. I've often asked: 'Why does everyone hate us ?'

ALEX FERGUSON.

It's better that they get rid of their frustrations here rather than going back home and taking it out on the wife, isn't it ? Or the wives taking them out on their husbands.

ALEX FERGUSON encouraging the fans to cheer the team on against Juventus in the 1996 Champions' League.

You care, care about the people who support you. At Manchester United you become one of them, you think like a supporter, suffer like a supporter.

ALEX FERGUSON.

There's something about Cantona which symbolises what the hard-core United fan feels about themselves. Like him, we're picked on and hated because we reckon we are the best. What he was saying with that kick was what we want to say: 'You cannot say that sort of thing to us and get away with it. We are United, respect us. '

JIM WHITE, journalist and United fan.

In Manchester the public is faithful, married for eternity to its players.

ERIC CANTONA.

FANS

Some of our supporters are happy to see us lose provided we score four goals and entertain them.

ALEX FERGUSON.

We are fortunate to have such a fine bunch of fans. They are very discerning and I believe they know their football as well as any supporters anywhere.

MATT BUSBY in 1961.

Perhaps the greatest nights of all for United supporters were the two floodlit FA Cup games with Sheffield Wednesday and West Bromwich after Munich. Then, roaring crowds of over 60,000 willed United to victory after one of the greatest exhibitions of mass encouragement ever known in Manchester's soccer history. Some called it hysteria, others said it was unhealthy, this incredible mob worship of one football team.

PETER MORRIS, journalist.

Tell the families it's nothing like *Midnight Express.*

A UNITED FAN who was held in jail in Turkey after United's match in the European Cup against Galatasaray in 1993.

When I watch United I get horny. If I weren't Red, I'd rather be dead.

BERNARD KEANE, a fan.

If you can get us to the final again next year, you can have my wife too.

A FAN to Tommy Docherty after it was revealed that he was having an affair with the wife of United's physiotherapist.

Their support has been an embarrassment at times, but I'd rather have them as an embarrassment than not at all.

TOMMY DOCHERTY.

SPEAK OF THE DEVILS

I took my little nephew to Old Trafford recently, he is only four and already has all the United gear, but being his first time at a live game and just seeing his face, I thought what a great thing that on a Saturday, for the rest of his life, whatever he decides to do, that he can go to relax and enjoy this amazing spectacle in this particular stadium.

JONATHAN MORRIS, actor.

I am trying to talk the producer into doing a tour of *Grease* in Europe so that I can follow Manchester United around.

SHANE RICHIE, television personality.

Eric signed my book, used my pen to sign everyone else's and then walked off with it. I prefer Ryan Giggs anyway.

MARIE HASSELLI, 13.

Every Friday night - that is whenever Manchester United are playing at home on the following afternoon - the boat is crammed with scarf-drenched Red Devils travelling to Old Trafford to pay homage. The only other occasion on which an Irish expedition on this scale is undertaken regularly is a pilgrimage to Lourdes. For them football represents one side of religion.

JOHN EDWARDS, journalist.

You can keep your trendy bistros on the King's Road, the smell of fish and chips mingled with success down Sir Matt Busby Way will sit nicely in my nostrils.

PETER BLYTHE, a fan.

The growing number of hospitality packages has brought in a different type of audience. They sit and admire the ground and can't wait to be entertained - just as if they were at a theatre or musical.

ALEX FERGUSON.

FANS

If Ince does get any stick from the United fans, he can look at his bank balance and I'm sure that will cheer him up.

NICKY BUTT after Paul Ince signed for Liverpool.

My mum's cooking pork chops on Wednesday - would you like to come round for tea ?

A FAN in a letter to Lee Sharpe.

I could almost have accepted it if he'd had another woman - but to lose your husband to a bunch of footballers is a joke.

EMMA MORGAN who cited her husband's fixation with Manchester United in their divorce.

Stick to Selling Sugar Puffs, Kev.

FAN'S BANNER after United won the 1996 Premiership title.

A quarter of a hour with supporters now and then is the least I can give them. In France I have often refused to sign autographs and I have gone so far as to criticise the public violently. There's no love there. No passion.

ERIC CANTONA.

In England everything is beautiful. The stadiums are beautiful, the atmosphere is beautiful, the cops on horseback are beautiful. The crowds respect you.

ERIC CANTONA.

Abroad, the crowd is too far from the players. Here the game is warmer. There is even room for love between the crowds and players. The crowd vibrates with the game.

ERIC CANTONA.

It's the biggest club in Norway.

OLE GUNNAR SOLKSJAER on United.

Eric was one of us. He loved the game.

ANDY WALSH, secretary of the Independent Manchester United Supporter's Association.

Eric is an idol
Eric is a star
If my mother had her way
He'd also be my Pa.

POEM by 13 year old fan Sebastian Pennells and his single-parent mum.

Seems I can't walk along the street without somebody wanting to know what it's all about at Old Trafford. Still, it's nice to meet mates, even if most of them are being met for the very first time.

GEORGE BEST.

I'm getting a right ribbing. It's embarrassing.

Todd McILWAIN who named his baby son Sparky two days before Mark Hughes signed for Chelsea.

Pack up your treble in your old kit bag.

SUPPORTER'S BANNER at the 1977 Cup Final when Liverpool where going for the treble of the League, the F.A.Cup and the European Cup.

Cantona rules the Evans.

BANNER at the 1996 FA Cup Final after United beat Liverpool to win the Double Double.

Yes we won the Double last year, but now we have to go one better and do something in Europe. It's for the fans to look back and boast about the latest victory, to go into work and have a go at other fans and feel proud.

GARY NEVILLE.

FANS

I think capital punishment is a great deterrent.

TOMMY DOCHERTY on football hooligans.

If we were United supporters, people would really f***ing hate us.
If we were a proper smug big band with pots of money and the
championship trophy and Alex Ferguson as manager, people'd go,
AAAAAAAAAAAAAAARGH ! I f***ing hate you.

NOEL GALLAGHER of Oasis.

We've got that Mickey Phelan
Woe-oh that Mickey Phelan
We've got that Mickey Phelan
And he's sub, sub, sub
Woe, woe, woe

SUPPORTER'S SONG sung to the tune of *You've Lost That Lovin'*
Feeling.

David James, superstar, drops more balls than Grobbelaar.

SUPPORTERS as United beat Liverpool 3-1 at Anfield in 1997.

Ooh Aah, Paul McGrath.

UNITED CHANT.

Ooh Aah, Cantona.

UNITED CHANT.

When the Reds score a goal
And it's not Andy Cole,
It's Poborsky.

**SONG by United fan Peter Boyle which goes to the tune of Dean
Martin's** *Amore.*

Merci pour Cantona, scum.

BANNER when Manchester United played Leeds United.

I'm at the merchandising mercy,
I've got every single jersey.
Of the red one I've got two.

MAN UNITED MAN, written by the Saw Doctors.

Hello Johnny Carey you can hear the girls all cry.
Hello Johnny Carey you're the apple of my eye.
You're a decent boy from Ireland there's no-one can deny,
You're a harum scarum divil-may-careum decent Irish boy.

SUPPORTER'S SONG.

You are my Solskjaer
My only Solskjaer
You make me happy
When skies are grey
And although Shearer was so much dearer
Please don't take my Ole away.

SONG in praise of Ole Gunnar Solskjaer to the tune of *You Are My Sunshine*.

Where are you now Georgie?
With those boots that laced up the side
And that Irish shirt you wore with pride
And that picture of you with Mike Summerbee and bride?
Where are you now, Georgie?
I dreamed of you dribbling past City's back four
And leaving Joe Corrigan fumbling on the floor
And the Stretford End singing ' More, Bestie more ! '

WHERE ARE YOU NOW, GEORGIE, song by Sportchestra.

Simply Red.

THE NAME United fanatic Mick Hucknall gave to his band

It's only in the last two years I've realised they're such a sexy team.

ZOE BALL, television personality.

FANS

United have been an obsession with me since the F.A.Cup final success against Leicester in 1963 and the golden days of Best, Law and Charlton. They were the team to watch. My dad took me to White Hart Lane to watch them against Tottenham and they closed the turnstiles with us two paces away. It took me months to get over that.

ANGUS DEAYTON, television personality.

Truly, I've never known anything like it. They idolise him. More than they did Denis Law, even more than they did George Best.

PAT CRERAND on Eric Cantona.

LOSING

Everyone in the place is on cloud nine. Well, perhaps by the time they come down they'll have lost the league again.

ALEX FERGUSON after United lost 5-0 at Newcastle in 1996.

The Cantona situation cost us everything.

ALEX FERGUSON after losing the 1995 F.A. Cup Final to Everton.

We created so many chances at the end that I wish I was still centre forward.

ALEX FERGUSON after the1-1 dreaw with West Ham which cost United the Premiership title in 1995.

You know, if we'd won the title this time, I think we'd never have lost it again.

PAT CRERAND after the same event.

I was driving to work and you see the kids smiling on their way to school. In your blinkered way you think how can they be enjoying themselves? What can there possibly be to smile about on a day like this? But you get over it..

ALEX FERGUSON the morning after United lost 1-0 to Fenerbahce in the Champions' League. It was United's first home defeat in 41 years of European competition.

I don't play against a particular team. I play to fight against the idea of losing.

ERIC CANTONA.

In the end we were accused of bottling it. I'm not admitting to that - but we've never made any excuses and I'm not going to start now.

STEVE BRUCE on losing the League title to Leeds in 1992.

Defeat at Bournemouth was a horrible experience. Funnily enough, we beat Barcelona not long after in the Cup Winner's Cup and I told Maradona that he could think himself lucky he hadn't been playing Bournemouth.

RON ATKINSON after United were knocked out of the FA Cup in 1984.

I used to come home in a hump if we got beat. Now I see Thomas smiling and it changes everything. There's only room for one baby in the house.

PAUL INCE.

Having worked so hard to get yourself through the rounds to the final, losing is one of the biggest disappointments you can feel in football. You feel devastated and totally drained, both physically and mentally. Last year was an experience that I never want to be faced with again.

DENNIS IRWIN after losing the 1995 FA Cup Final.

You know things never go on forever and at some point, some time..... But if it's going to happen I hope it's long after I'm in the big penalty box in the sky, in peace.

ALEX FERGUSON on United's unbeaten home record in Europe.

Some setbacks don't just numb you, they smack you right between the eyes and leave a vacuum in your life, a void that just seems inescapable.

ALEX FERGUSON after United failed to win the Championship in 1992.

Too many of our players thought all they had to do was turn up to collect their medals. And they did - losers medals.

MARTIN BUCHAN on United's Cup Final defeat against Southampton in 1976

To lose after that was like winning the pools only to find you'd forgotten to post the coupon.

SAMMY McILROY after United's last minute F.A. Cup Final defeat by Arsenal in 1978.

It beats the trip City fans made to Port Vale this week.

A FAN after United lost 1-0 to Juventus in Turin in the Champions' League in 1996.

I have never come across the situation we had in the closing weeks of that season. Our failure seemed to make a lot of people very happy. I find it difficult to understand. It is bitter and twisted.

ALEX FERGUSON reflecting on United's near miss for the title in 1992.

I have seldom felt so depressed in my life as I did that weekend.

DENIS LAW after scoring the goal for Manchester City that sent United into the Second Division.

We murdered Everton - it could have been 22-4. They had three chances and scored four.

RON ATKINSON after United lost 4-2 to Everton.

I'm not making any complaints. Anyway, we always try to make it nice and difficult for ourselves, to give the rest a bit of hope. That's the really Christian thing to do.

ALEX FERGUSON after losing to Southampton in early 1998.

MANAGERS

It will be all down-hill for him from now on. Leaving Manchester United is like leaving the Hilton and booking in at some run-down little hotel round the corner.

TOMMY DOCHERTY after Ron Atkinson was sacked.

He came a stranger and left a stranger.

DENIS LAW on Frank O'Farrell.

I have been punished for falling in love.

TOMMY DOCHERTY who was sacked for his affair with the wife of club physiotherapist Laurie Brown.

The thing that got him sacked wasn't the falling in love - it was making the physio reserve team manager, sending him on scouting trips and giving his wife one while he was away.

WILLIE MORGAN.

If something happens over the weekend, are you interested in coming to Old Trafford ?

MATT BUSBY'S first approach to Tommy Docherty about becoming manager of United.

You can have my home number, but please remember not to call during *The Sweeney*.

RON ATKINSON to journalists after he was appointed boss of United.

No, I am not a Catholic - but I'm willing to be converted.

RON ATKINSON, the first non Roman Catholic manager at United for over 30 years, after his appointment.

I've had to swap my Merc for a BMW, I'm down to my last 37 suits and I'm drinking non-vintage champagne.

RON ATKINSON after being dismissed by Manchester United.

I believe you are seeking a team manager? Well, I am interested.

MATT BUSBY to the United Chairman in 1945.

Whatever personal honours have come my way would not have been possible without the magnificent help of all connected with Old Trafford from directors right through to gatemen. The honours are theirs as much as mine.

MATT BUSBY after completing 21 years as manager of United.

I always felt that my destiny lay at Old Trafford. Now the chance to manage the biggest club in British football was there for the taking. I didn't need a second prompting. I told the United director I would walk from Scotland to Old Trafford for the job.

TOMMY DOCHERTY.

I love to see them doing well. United is still my club at heart and I would have walked back and worked for nothing if I had been given a second chance.

TOMMY DOCHERTY.

Football management these days is like nuclear war - no winners, just survivors

TOMMY DOCHERTY.

Ten years here is worth is worth 30 anywhere else.

ALEX FERGUSON.

MANAGERS

I don't know how many managers have lost their jobs this season but I know all of us have faced anxiety at one stage or another. But if you put us all together I doubt whether the pressure would match up to what Alex [Ferguson] has faced.

BRIAN CLOUGH speaking in 1990.

One man stopped me winning the championship for Manchester United. Not once, but three times. His name? Ian Rush.

RON ATKINSON.

Jock Stein once told me that he turned down the job with United and he regretted it all his life. I am determined not to miss the chance. I feel dreadful about leaving Aberdeen after such a marvellous time with them.

ALEX FERGUSON after becoming United's manager.

But it still hurts deep down and the anguish of losing this job won't disappear in a long time. Nobody wants to leave United whether they are the boss or the teaboy.

RON ATKINSON.

Old Trafford is a theatre for entertainment, drama and football spectacle. It's not a stadium where you should hear bellyaching or fans bickering about their own team. That just destroys the magic of the place.

RON ATKINSON.

It was easier for the Board of Directors to sack the manager than 20 players. And it is the players who must shoulder some of the responsibility for the boss going.

JESPER OLSEN after Ron Atkinson was sacked.

They can take my job away, but they can't rob me of my ability.

TOMMY DOCHERTY after being sacked by United.

Win, lose or draw, this is better than working down the pit.

MATT BUSBY.

It was afterwards that I realised how much bigger the job was than I'd thought. Only when you are outside do you see that everyone is talking about Manchester United more than any other club. You think: ' My God, were they doing that when I was here? '

WILF McGUINNESS.

A death by a thousand cuts.

FRANK O'FARRELl, describing his treatment as manager at Old Trafford.

I had never admired a man as much as Matt Busby. But when I left Old Trafford I had never been let down by any man as much as by him.

FRANK O'FARRELL.

Right, Ron, now what kind of car were you thinking of driving ?

Well Mr .Chairman, at West Bromwich I had a Mercedes 450sl and I was very impressed with the comfort and reliability.

Dave Sexton had a Rover.

Mr. Chairman, I have a dog called Charlie but I thought we were talking about motorcars not dogs.

MARTIN EDWARDS AND RON ATKINSON.

When I was offered the job I was both thrilled and flattered, but I could not help feeling that Manchester United and Ron Atkinson were made for each other.

RON ATKINSON.

I will not be just United's manager. I will be an ardent fan. If the team bores me, it will be boring supporters who hero-worship the players. I will not allow these people to be betrayed.

RON ATKINSON.

It is time for action at Old Trafford. Others may have been frightened off before me but I have not.

RON ATKINSON.

I have always said the biggest stage is the best place to entertain. That means Frank Sinatra at Carnegie Hall, Richard Burton at the Old Vic and Manchester United at Old Trafford.

RON ATKINSON.

To my mind this job is bigger and tougher than managing England.

RON ATKINSON.

For 18 years I have been devoted to United. Now I must find a future away from Old Trafford.

WILF McGUINNESS.

The sacking of Ron Atkinson is the best thing that could happen to Manchester United and it didn't come a day too soon. I don't like to see any manager get the sack, but I can't say I feel sorry because I hate the man. His downfall has been all his own doing. I dislike him because of his flash personality.

TOMMY DOCHERTY.

Your self-belief must never waver. I think there were attacks on me because of my nature. Sometimes I knock everything out of the road to get what I want. I had an energy to do that and a determination which is the most essential part of me.

ALEX FERGUSON.

This is the job I've always wanted. It's the job everyone in football wants.

FRANK O'FARRELL.

United is everyone's second love

FRANK O'FARRELL.

Look, I left Bobby Charlton out of the side. Fair enough, I expected some reaction with a player as popular as Bobby involved. But the letters I got. They came from all over the world. And all telling me I was wrong. That's when you realise how many people are looking at you when you get a reaction like that.

FRANK O'FARRELL.

Not everyone, sadly, would play for Wilf. The side as a whole did not give a one hundred per cent effort for him. As soon as Sir Matt returned to the scene it changed at once.

DAVID SADLER who played in the 1960s and 1970s

It is a long time since we offered sacrificial lambs in this country, but [Wilf] McGuinness was virtually one. From the day he took over he never had a chance.

BRIAN CLOUGH.

Under Ron Atkinson, life was demanding but more relaxed. Where he would yell at you if you stepped out of line and give you another final warning, the new boss will steam in first time and hit you with everything he's got.

PAUL McGRATH on Alex Ferguson

There was no doubt he had a big ego. We would not see him for most of the week but if the cameras were there he would turn up and have his hair groomed so that he looked his best.

FRANK STAPLETON on Ron Atkinson.

Being the flamboyant character that he is didn't really suit the Manchester public, the people on the terraces who are basically working class. To them there was always the belief that Ron Atkinson was a big-headed bastard. He was flash and they didn't enjoy that.

NOEL CANTWELL, who captained the 1963 F.A. Cup winning team

Frank O'Failure.

NEWSPAPER headline.

As far as he is concerned he is a God. There's nobody big enough to tell him what to do.

MARGARET ATKINSON on her husband Ron.

There can be few managers who have lost their job after seven consecutive victories.

DAVE SEXTON after he was sacked as boss of United.

This person suffers from erotic fantasies. He thinks a lot about sex, though he is very devoted to his mother.

GRAPHOLOGIST'S analysis of Ron Atkinson's handwriting

Alex Ferguson is a great manager

KENNY DALGLISH.

I would bleed for United, though this is disappointing. But managers are judged by results, yet with a bit of luck we might have been in three cup finals.

WILF McGUINNESS.

After becoming a cardinal in this cathedral who could go back to being a parish priest ?

TOMMY DOCHERTY.

It was not an easy assignment. The ground had been blitzed, they had an overdraft at the bank, and what is more I had no experience as a manager and I felt they were taking a great risk in appointing me. All I had, apart from playing experience, was ideas about what a manager should do, faith in those ideas and faith in the future of the club.

MATT BUSBY.

I am not resigning. I am not being sacked and there is neither trouble nor panic in our camp.

MATT BUSBY during a bad patch in 1951.

I am biased where Tommy [Docherty] is concerned and I make no apology for it. To me, the man is magic.

WILLIE MORGAN.

He's about the worst manager there's ever been and nearly all United fans will be delighted when he goes.

WILLIE MORGAN on Tommy Docherty.

I would hate to be the man who has to follow Matt Busby as manager of United.

JOE MERCER.

Came as a boy and left as an old man.

TONY DUNNE on Wilf McGuinness.

If ever a man was tailor-made to be manager of Manchester United it was Tommy Docherty, and it was as though all his earlier years of management in the game had been spent preparing for this one particular job.

STEVE COPPELL.

MANAGERS

I gave the club the FA Cup. They gave me the sack.

TOMMY DOCHERTY.

I've got to be honest and say the image of Manchester United overawed me, to a certain extent, but this job has got to be the peak of ambition for any manager.

DAVE SEXTON on his appointment.

I feel awkward saying: 'we'll murder 'em, ' and those kind of things. This is a dangerous game to go around boasting in.

DAVE SEXTON.

Come on, my bonny boys.

DAVE SEXTON'S last words to his team as they took the field.

There is something awesome about Old Trafford.

DAVE SEXTON.

He may not be the greatest manager in the game, but I haven't met a finer bloke.

BRYAN ROBSON on Ron Atkinson.

When Fergie has a verbal blast, it can be measured on the Richter Scale.

MARK HUGHES.

You can't go into a club and tell people their fitness is terrible, that they're bevvying, they're playing too much golf, and their ground is filthy. You simply have to improve things bit by bit.

ALEX FERGUSON.

I have tried to pay back Alex Ferguson in kind. Him and my teammates.

ERIC CANTONA.

Who is your favourite manager ?

The manager of Stringfellows.

GEORGE BEST during a question and answer session.

After ten years I might know the manager quite well but I still don't know how he picks his teams.

BRIAN McCLAIR.

He was a breath of fresh air.

KEVIN MORAN on the arrival of Alex Ferguson as manager.

It's one of the things I wish to God I'd had the opportunity of doing - being manager of Manchester United

NOEL CANTWELL.

The chairman should never say: 'If we don't win the league, the manager's out.' You have to judge things like that at the end of the season.

MARTIN EDWARDS, Manchester United's Chief Executive.

Managers are honest, marvellous people a lot of the time. But we all tell lies. Any manager who is not honest enough to admit that is the biggest liar of them all.

TOMMY DOCHERTY.

All this talk about Tommy Docherty not being fit to run a football club is rubbish. That's exactly what he is fit for.

CLIVE JAMES, writer and broadcaster.

MANAGERS

When the television people asked me to play a football manager in a film, I asked how long it would take. They said about ten days and I said: 'About par for the course. '

TOMMY DOCHERTY.

He's the only manager who can hold a serious, face-to-face conversation and tell you what's happening 20 yards behind him.

TOMMY CAVANAGH, United coach, on Tommy Docherty.

He has this paternal attitude to the younger players. He goes out of his way to guide and look after them.

PETER SCHMEICHEL on Alex Ferguson.

They say management is all about making decisions and it took me just four months to decide I wasn't cut out for it.

MARTIN BUCHAN who managed Burnley after he retired.

You can have the best collection of footballers ever, but if there is no-one driving the bus, you'll not get there.

ALEX FERGUSON.

Big Ron From Old Swan Signs On

MESSAGE on T-shirts doing the rounds of Liverpool after Ron Atkinson was sacked. Atkinson comes from the Old Swan area of Liverpool.

Good day for a hanging.

FRANK O'FARRELL as he arrived at Old Trafford on the day he was sacked.

He's so greedy for success if his grandkids beat him at cards he sends them to bed without any supper.

GARY PALLISTER on Alex Ferguson.

I can say it's the most we ever spent on a sports book. But this is going to be the best-selling sports book ever published. We all knew this was the big one.

RODDY BLOOMFIELD, publisher at Hodder & Stoughton, after the deal to publish Alex Ferguson's biography.

Years ago Man United used to lose to Wimbledon nine times out of ten because they weren't man enough for the job. What Fergie has done brilliantly is to put together a skilful squad and a squad that can fight and tackle, fight and be nasty. Not nasty, nasty, but aggressive in the right context.

BARRY FRY.

It's the ultimate pressure job, but you know that and I'm delighted I accepted although I got the sack in the end.

DAVE SEXTON.

United's list of signings from our City ground reads like a Who's Who. Perhaps United haven't signed the one who could have sorted them out once and for all. I'm referring to Old Big Head here. I'm long in the tooth. I've got middle-age spread and, quite frankly, one way or another I've shot it now. But if someone at Old Trafford had the courage, conviction or whatever it needed over the years to say: 'let's go and get Cloughie', who knows what might have happened.

BRIAN CLOUGH.

I want to manage a massive club. If the Manchester United job becomes available, I'll apply for it.

JOE KINNEAR.

MEDIA

I might go to Alcoholics Anonymous but I think it would be difficult for me to remain anonymous.

GEORGE BEST.

I think I have already doubled the number of interviews I've ever done in the last couple of weeks. I never used to think I had anything interesting to say, but if I'm captain of Manchester United I must have, mustn't I?

ROY KEANE.

When I look at the way United protect Ryan Giggs from the media and everything else, I wonder if that might have helped. There is a lot of advice for stars like Ryan, but I don't know. If they had told me how to behave I would probably have done the opposite.

GEORGE BEST.

Don't buy the papers and then you don't have to read what is written. You could get paranoid about it, obsessed with some of them, but when you are the manager of Manchester United you need a thick skin and can't allow comments from supporters to upset you.

ALEX FERGUSON.

I've done a few interviews now. And you learn; it's like football, you get better as you do it.

RYAN GIGGS.

A lot of the lads tell me when they're on holiday they spend their time on the beach reading about me.

RYAN GIGGS.

He's more Albert Square than Rover's Return, more pie and mash than Betty's Hot Pot.

THE DAILY STAR on David Beckham.

I don't want to be on the front pages. I want to be on the back.

DAVID BECKHAM.

I was God's gift to the press, wasn't I? I used to start sounding off and they'd say: 'Hold on Tom, we can't get it all down.' So I'd say the same outrageous things, only slower.

TOMMY DOCHERTY.

Everyone makes mistakes - mine just seem to get more publicity than other people's.

GEORGE BEST.

They don't get read in my house. That's just the way I am. Apart from rare praise, I know what they are going to say about me beforehand. I don't need them to rub my nose in it. I just don't talk to them, so they write what they want anyway.

ANDY COLE on newspapers.

Stop reading the papers.

MATT BUSBY'S advice to Alex Ferguson when he was getting a hard time from the papers.

MISBEHAVING

All I could see was the ball. I thought I had a 50-50 chance of getting it.

KEVIN MORAN on the tackle that led him to be the first player to be sent off in an F.A. Cup Final.

I shudder to think what might have happened outside had we been beaten.

RON ATKINSON on the same event.

A lot of people are afraid to ask me about being sent off in that match. What they forget about is that it never really bothered me being sent off because we won the game. If we had lost the game I think that even now I'd feel a bit sick.

KEVIN MORAN.

I don't think that because someone is sent off in a Cup Final he should be regarded as a total embarrassment to the game. But that is how I felt.

KEVIN MORAN.

My decision was correct and I haven't had any second thoughts since. I sent him off for serious foul play. That is the law of the game. The circumstances and importance of the match did not come into it. I would have made the same decision in any game.

PETER WILLIS who sent off Kevin Moran in the 1985 Cup Final.

Norman's goal really lifted us. It was a brilliant goal and in many ways when I look back on the final, even though my dismissal got a lot of coverage, it was a shame really because the whole thing about the game should have been Norman's.

KEVIN MORAN.

I don't care if he's George Best or Pele. Unless he's willing to do hard training, he won't get a look in.

MALCOLM HOLMAN, manager of the Ford Open Prison football team, after George Best's arrival.

I would have cut off his testicles.

BRIAN CLOUGH on Eric Cantona's attack on Matthew Simmons.

We are no longer interested in his escapades, his pseudo-philosophical bragging, his crudeness and the state of his soul. He lives his life and we live ours. And we don't miss him

LE PROVENCAL, French newspaper, on Eric Cantona.

Eric Cantona is the Darth Vader of football, a brilliant genius whose soul is infected by malignity.

ROB KING, journalist.

He has had more red cards than football clubs: no mean feat when one considers he has been at eight clubs.

JOHN MULLIN, journalist, on Eric Cantona.

Call it arrogance, call it craziness, call it petulance. But Cantona is Cantona. Like me, outbursts such as this are in the blood. I never went looking for trouble and I'm sure Eric doesn't either. Trouble just finds you.

DENIS LAW after Eric Cantona's attack on Matthew Simmons.

MISBEHAVING

George Best was provoked all the time but he handled it. We were brought up to believe that when playing for Manchester United you don't worry about the crowd.

ALEX STEPNEY reacting to Eric Cantona's attack on Matthew Simmons.

Crystal Palace should take a long and hard look at their security or rather the lack of it.

PAT CRERAND on the same event.

I suppose my crime sheet makes me appear to be something of an old lag. It's certainly nothing to boast about. But all my sins have been in retaliation. I've never been a dirty player. Perhaps I've been too easily provoked, like many Scots.

PAT CRERAND.

When the boss calls you into his office you know you're for it. He doesn't hand out the toffees.

NOBBY STILES on Matt Busby.

I'll never change my game. It isn't possible. If I did I wouldn't be half the player I am. I'd be back in Irish football. I'll obviously be sent off a few more times. It's part and parcel of the game.

ROY KEANE.

Everyone said that because I was picking up so many bookings last season it was because I was getting slower. That wasn't true. If I got any slower I'd have come to a standstill.

STEVE BRUCE.

George Best had been felled by a full-back who was noted for his ability to get in a really tough tackle. The referee gave the defender a ticking-off. The culprit answered back: ' what else do you expect me to do? He's making me look a right idiot '

ALEX STEPNEY.

Denis [Law] once kicked me at Wembley in front of the Queen in an international. I mean, no man is entitled to do that, really.

BOBBY ROBSON.

If someone went through and I could catch him by bringing him down, I'd bring him down. If I didn't, I'd feel I had let my team-mates and my fans down.

BRYAN ROBSON.

He reminds me of [Bryan] Robson in many ways but does not have the control in the tackle in terms of not getting booked. Robbo would get away with murder and even argue with refs - he was good at that. Roy can't. Robbo had it down to a fine art and withdrew before the ref reached for his card. Roy carries on and gets the card.

ALEX FERGUSON on Roy Keane.

It's shameful - poor Eric might as well commit suicide.

ELEANORE CANTONA, Eric's Mum, after he received a two-week prison sentence.

It would take a brave manager to instruct his players not to commit what has become known as the 'professional foul .'

WILF McGUINNESS.

We are no longer prepared to tolerate his wayward behaviour. If he got married and settled down, it would help somewhat. But his present behaviour has got to stop. One thing we have to understand is that George Best is a genius. The problem is that he has had as much adulation as Pele of Brazil and he got it very young. He has been continually hounded by the press and public alike and his weakness for a pretty girl has not helped the situation.

MATT BUSBY.

Hopefully, I won't be sent off as captain, but if I was a betting man, I wouldn't have much money on that.

ROY KEANE.

Hard men are nothing new in football. In my young days there were quite a few killers about, men who went in for rough play and intimidation. But you wouldn't expect one team to have more than a couple of them. What is new and frightening about the present situation is that you have entire sides that have physical hardness as their main asset.

MATT BUSBY in 1969.

We can't all be a Bobby Charlton.

ALEX FERGUSON on his own temperament.

I never damaged anybody intentionally. A lot of fouls awarded against me were intended tackles. I was just too slow when I got there.

NORMAN WHITESIDE.

The Boss never has to say anything. If any member of the staff does anything wrong, the other players are so ashamed of him because he has let down the Boss, that the lad goes along and apologises.

JACK CROMPTON, who played in the 1940s and 50s.

We are constantly told we have to be role models and we accept the responsibility. But players are only human and at some stage you are going to crack.

GARY PALLISTER.

I don't think anyone in the history of football will get the sentence Eric got...unless they had killed Bert Millichip's dog.

ALEX FERGUSON on Eric Cantona's eight-month ban by the FA.

I was up in his office a few times when I was a kid and he could be stern. You didn't mess about with him, but I think he liked a bit of devilment. He'd be telling you off, but he'd have a glint in his eye.

NOBBY STILES on Matt Busby.

I definitely think we were unfairly treated over Cantona and Keane. It makes me laugh when people go on about so-called incidents our players have been involved in this past year and you see some of the tackles that go on in other games. There's not been one broken nose, broken jaw, cut, gash, knee ligament injury or even a bled wart, not a flippin' thing as a result of our players' tackles.

ALEX FERGUSON.

Eric [Cantona] stamped on me and was sent off but I'd still pay to watch him play.

JOHN MONCUR.

I've been punished for striking a goalkeeper. For spitting at supporters. For throwing my shirt at a referee. For calling my manager a bag of shit. I called those who judged a bunch of idiots. I thought I might have trouble finding a sponsor.

ERIC CANTONA in an advertisement for Nike.

Wasn't it good to see Eric Cantona back in action? Let's hope this time he remembers that kicking people in the teeth is the Tory government's job.

TONY BLAIR MP.

I was free to paint and to live with my wife Isabelle and my dogs. But it was also time for experiments. I shaved my head to feel the fresh rain and the strength of the wind on my skull.... I was at liberty to begin a session of psychoanalysis without being called a madman.

ERIC CANTONA on his activities during his eight month ban.

How does a man of such aesthetic refinement - poet, philosopher, painter and penalty-taker end up with a worse disciplinary record than Vinnie Jones? Perhaps the question would only be asked in England, where intellectuals aren't expected to 'engage' in rough-and-tumble - fighting duels, committing crimes of passion or hurling cobblestones at riot police.

FRANCIS WHEEN, journalist.

It is fortunate that most players are not like me or there would be anarchy.

ERIC CANTONA.

It's my nature to react the way I do. It's an instinct and to hell with people who are not happy with it.

ERIC CANTONA.

I hear now and again from certain managers that you have to be a killer to succeed. Myself, I have never killed anyone.

ERIC CANTONA.

When Eric [Cantona] feels an injustice, he has to prove to the whole world that he's been wronged. He can't control his temper. That's just part of his game.

ALEX FERGUSON.

Given Cantona's intellectuality, perhaps the surest way to wind him up would be to challenge him on a philosophical basis. It may well turn out, in the fullness of time, that what [Matthew] Simmons actually shouted was: Eric! Your concept of individuality is grossly diluted! You fail to acknowledge the despair pendant upon the absurdity of the human predicament! Abandon your semi-consciousness! You're acquiescent and you know you are ! Come and have a go if you think you're Sartian enough !

GILES SMITH, journalist.

Neutrals are now insisting we should have one extreme of Eric without the other: the Thinker without the Thug, the Rimbaud without the Rambo side of Eric Cantona. There's no chance of that. For every back heel that makes a goal, there will always be one aimed at someone's face.

JIM SHELLEY, fan.

Cantona Free, Philosophy Nil.

DAILY TELEGRAPH headline after Eric Cantona's famous seagulls quote.

This has been a love story. It is something that is very strong for me. The love of the club is the most important weapon in the world. I just couldn't leave.

ERIC CANTONA dismissing suggestions that he might leave United.

Do they seriously think I don't want to change? Of course I do! But I can't change. I know myself well enough to realise I can't promise to change. I can only try and go on trying. I can get whacked from the back or hit when the ball has gone 28 times in a row and do nothing or say nothing. I don't know why it should boil the 29th time, which has been no different. It just happens.

GEORGE BEST.

A lot of rubbish is talked about destroyers and tough defenders. I call them dirty bastards.

GEORGE BEST.

What Best didn't realise until it was too late was that whereas Paul McCartney could stay up until the small hours and then write a pop song about it, George simply found it more difficult to keep himself at a level of fitness required in a top athlete.

MICHAEL PARKINSON, writer and broadcaster.

George Best, sadly, was the little boy who never grew up. Tomorrow he is 26, yet he is little more mature than the day he left Belfast for Old Trafford. He has been his own worst enemy so often and he has never learned from his mistakes.

DAVID MILLER, journalist, in 1972.

Why can't he have been like Tom Finney ?

JOHN ANTHONY, journalist, on George Best.

'Tragedy' is a greatly devalued word, as often applied to an own goal as an earthquake. But when you think of Manchester United and George Best and when you consider the sheer pleasure which they and he used to offer us, it becomes impossible to by-pass the word.

JOHN ANTHONY.

When he's boozing he's the most deplorable, obnoxious, sarcastic, ignorant, horrible piece of rubbish.

ANGIE BEST in 1982.

Let's get the record straight. I've never seen George [Best] the worse for drink. He doesn't smoke and he does train hard.

BOBBY CHARLTON.

If a fellow has to kick me it means he is not as good as I am.

GEORGE BEST.

All my lot can stay out until four every morning if they can play half as well as George.

A FOOTBALL MANAGER on George Best.

Try not to foul.

ERIC CANTONA while training youngsters.

I feel I'm probably on probation at present at the club. The manager probably doesn't trust me 100 per cent. I haven't been sent off yet but we've only had two games so far. Give me time, you never know.

ROY KEANE after he was made captain.

Nobby Stiles doesn't so much tackle people as bump into them.

BOBBY CHARLTON.

Because I was born with fair hair and a face something like a cross between Tommy Steele and Danny Kaye people may think I'm incapable of being down in the dumps. They don't know me. I am being very serious indeed when I say that my suspension last season was sheer disaster for me. What made it worse was that I knew I deserved to be suspended.

DENIS LAW in 1964.

People try this case like it was the worst case in the world. Of course sport is not a fight, it's to make friends. He has to be punished but not banished from football.

PELE on Eric Cantona.

We were probably playing against the world, Mars and everyone else tonight.

ALEX FERGUSON after Eric Cantona was sent off for the second time in four days in the 2-2 draw at Arsenal.

With me it goes one, three, seven and bump.

BRIAN KIDD on his inability to count to ten when the atmosphere becomes heated.

It's the first time, after a match, that we've had to replace divots in the players.

RON ATKINSON after a violent encounter with Valencia.

MISBEHAVING

The drinking, gambling and discos used to amaze me. Players would ask me why I didn't join them for lunch after training. Well, I can tell you these sorts of lunches didn't involve much eating.

ARNOLD MUHREN.

I have no regrets about it. I did what I did for the rest of the team.

OLE GUNNAR SOLSKJAER after being sent off for bringing down Newcastle's Robert Lee.

MONEY

Manchester United take more in programme sales than we take on the gate.

LAWRIE McMENEMY.

Money has not been my motive. I think I'm sentimental about football. I would rather tell my children about the medals I've won and the goals I scored than how much I earned.

BOBBY CHARLTON.

I never thought the day would come when I would be paid to wear sports gear.

RYAN GIGGS after signing a deal with Reebok.

United were bad payers in the 1970s. I think they had the mentality that footballers would play for them for nothing. People moan about agents but I wish they'd been around in my day.

STUART PEARSON.

Money in the bank is no use to a football team. You have to put your money on the field where the public can see it.

MATT BUSBY.

I spent a lot of money on booze, birds and fast cars. The rest I just squandered.

GEORGE BEST.

MONEY

The stadium has certainly changed a lot since my day and they never had raffles to give away £4,000 when I was a player up there. We could only dream about being paid that much in my day.

LOU MACARI.

Less than a month after thousands of youngsters pulled on their favourite club jersey at Christmas, the men who run the club ordered the Red Devils to trot out in blue at Southampton. Loyalty doesn't seem to be enough any more. Rather, it is exploited to make us pay more.

TONY BLAIR, MP.

If he's looking for a beacon to see how a club can be run, he should be looking at Manchester United and not making cheap shots.

KEN RAMSDEN, United's Assistant Secretary, replying to Blair.

Today's players would leave us for dead. They deserve whatever money they get.

JOHNNY CAREY, captain of the first great Busby team.

OOPS!

Tell Alex [Ferguson] we're coming to get him.

KEVIN KEEGAN after Newcastle United won promotion.

You don't win anything with kids.

ALAN HANSEN at the beginning of the 1995/96 season in which United won the Double Double.

I regard the game as a near certainty. Our team are in their best shape and getting ready to strike a mortal blow to Manchester's hopes.

MARIO COLUNA, Benfica captain, before the 1968 European Cup Final.

It will need an awful lot of bad luck for my team to return home defeated. If this does happen, then it will demonstrate that football follows an inhuman logic.

MARIO COLUNA.

I am hurt and upset by what is happening. Alex is destroying United. We'd love to praise Alex. But what has he given us in over three years ?

TOMMY DOCHERTY in 1990.

My conviction that by the time I retire I will have won all the major prizes the game has to offer has never wavered.

RON ATKINSON.

OOPS!

We are going to beat them to the championship. You have to feel sympathy for the way United missed out this season, but it was good for us because it now gives us the chance to get there before them. We were the last Manchester club to finish as champions and we'll be the next.

PETER SWALES, then Manchester City Chairman, in May 1992.

Manchester United has rubbed off on me. I feel its glamour already. I feel, too, a great need to help the club back to its famed and feared reputation.

FRANK O'FARRELL.

United's participation was not in the best interests of the League.

THE FOOTBALL LEAGUE on United's early European games.

Eric Cantona was sold to Manchester United because of a vision I couldn't get out of my mind. It kept repeating itself - the sight of the Frenchman disappearing over the horizon astride his Harley-Davidson with paint brushes and easel strapped on his back. It is an illusion that might yet come to haunt Alex Ferguson at Old Trafford.

HOWARD WILKINSON, then manager of Leeds United, after he sold Cantona.

Whoever happens to be the manager would be well advised to keep an ear cocked for the sound of the revving motorbike.

HOWARD WILKINSON.

I've had my ups and downs with Alex [Ferguson], but I do believe that overall he's been a fine boss at Old Trafford. I know he'll be haunted by the ghost of Mark Robins, the lad he let go to shoot Norwich to the top of the Premier League.

TOMMY DOCHERTY.

They're waiting to crown new kings out there. Get out and take the chance.

FRANK O'FARRELl to Ted MacDougall as he made his United debut.

He has a lot of things going for him ability wise. He's already ahead of say, Martin Chivers as an all-round player in my view: if not in close control then with his greater knowledge of the game, his greater appreciation of what to do in quick situations that demand quick thinking and awareness.

JOHN BOND, manager, on Ted MacDougall.

Sharp are currently working on bringing 3D TV into your living rooms. Mr. .Koshima [Managing Director] hopes it will be so realistic that viewers will have to duck when Eric Cantona takes a shot.

PRESS RELEASE from Sharp Electronics.

With due respect to United, I thought Liverpool should have won the title last season.

PAUL INCE as he signed for Liverpool in 1997.

They are just another English club. It doesn't make any difference if we are playing Sheffield United or Manchester United. All English teams play the same way.

RONALD KOEMAN, the Barcelona sweeper, before the European Cup Winner's Cup Final against United in 1991.

[Alan] Brazil is to goalscoring what Bryan Robson is to midfield play.

RON ATKINSON.

[Jesper] Olsen will, I feel certain, become the biggest playing sensation at Old Trafford since George Best.

RON ATKINSON.

OOPS!

I was up at Old Trafford not long ago and sat in Fergie's seat in that sort of podium thing he's had built overlooking the pitch, and, I thought: 'That's for me.'

MARK McGHEE.

Fergie, Fergie, on the dole.

UNITED SUPPORTERS after losing 3-0 to Aston Villa in 1989.

Fergie Out!

THE FIRST FRONT COVER HEADLINE in Red Issue, the Manchester United fanzine which appeared in February 1989

Three years of excuses: ta ta Fergie.

BANNER held aloft by fans after Alex Ferguson had been manager for three years.

I hope Cole scores bucketfuls of goals for United, but deep down I have my doubts.

GEORGE GRAHAM who sold Andy Coles while boss of Arsenal.

PRESSURE

It was a time of Merseyside domination and United were desperate for the title. The competition for places was incredible and even in training you had to be your best. You always felt you had to impress. I'm normally very laid back and when it came to a game, bang, I would try to prove my worth. But the pressure was so great on a daily basis that I would be drained even before a game.

ALAN BRAZIL recalling his time at United.

I used to look at Gordon McQueen who would throw up on the pitch actually before the kick-off with nerves and I knew how he felt. I used to relish matches away from Old Trafford. My record was actually pretty good - 25 games, 12 goals - but most of the goals were away from home, which is crazy.

ALAN BRAZIL.

This club is a nightmare. Every manager would want the job, but it can suck you in and take you over if you let it.

ALEX FERGUSON.

Wimbledon players ask you the question all the time: 'Are you as brave as I am ?' You have to prove that to them.

ALEX FERGUSON

The real pressure is when a lad at Rochdale has been given a free transfer.

RON ATKINSON.

PRESSURE

I'm careful of the players I lay into. Some can't handle it. Some can't even handle a team talk. There are some I don't look in the eye during a team talk because I know I'm putting them under pressure.

ALEX FERGUSON.

We've never resorted to that. You simply don't say things like he did in this game. I have kept really quiet but, I tell you something, he went down in my estimation after that and I'll tell him this - we're still fighting for this title. He has got to go to Middlesbrough and get something. And I tell you honestly, I would love it if we beat them now - absolutely love it.

KEVIN KEEGAN wilting under the pressure at the end of the 1995/96 season.

I don't lose sleep over our troubles. I went through the insomnia thing years ago when I was at Weymouth and we were near the bottom of the Southern League.

FRANK O'FARRELL.

I have taught myself to get away from it all mentally. It's a fantastic gift. And it's something I didn't have when I arrived here. Then I was completely consumed by the job. It ruled every moment of every day - and my sleeping hours too.

ALEX FERGUSON.

I don't have many regrets. If there is one big one, it is leaving United as early as I did because I could have become a multi-millionaire. Too bad, but at the time I just couldn't handle it. The pressure was too much for me.

GEORGE BEST.

You feel you have to be brilliant all the time.

DAVID BECKHAM.

SPEAK OF THE DEVILS

If I had paid attention to letters from fans at that time it would have been easy to sack him, but close to the club we knew all the sound things he was building for the future and we believed it was only a matter of time before things came right.

MARTIN EDWARDS on Alex Ferguson during a bad patch.

The singular fact that drives us Scots is fear of failure and a compelling determination to succeed. We cross the border into England to prove ourselves

ALEX FERGUSON.

They tax you, our team, don't they ? They make you work for your money. I should be paid £1 million a year for this job.

ALEX FERGUSON after the drawn F.A. Cup Final against Crystal Palace.

Alex is a canny old Scot, all right. He knows all about playing mind games. He's putting out the bowl of milk for us but we're not going to lap it up. He's a master at psyching people out. But psychology won't work on us. We've got too many psychos in the squad.

JOE KINNEAR after Alex Ferguson praised Wimbledon.

I don't like the pressure of playing for Manchester United, it's too much for me.

MICKEY THOMAS.

It's great to be on the pitch, that's when you feel the least pressure.

ROY KEANE.

There's a hell of a lot of politics in football. I don't think Henry Kissinger would have lasted 48 hours at Old Trafford.

TOMMY DOCHERTY.

PRESSURE

I could strangle all the people who have a go. The pressures that are on him are terrible. People invade his privacy and give him no breathing space. What people don't realise is that he is shy and bashful. You couldn't meet a nicer bloke. Don't forget it was the public who created the image.

TERRY NEILL on George Best.

They tell me to do so many things, so many bloody things: shave off my beard, cut my hair - as if that would make me into what they wanted me to be. Jesus Christ had a beard and long hair and they didn't want to change him.

GEORGE BEST.

They say that he'll be burned out by the time he is in his mid-20s, that no one can live at the pace he does. Well, I've played alongside him now for a long time now and I've seen nothing to suggest this.

BOBBY CHARLTON on George Best.

We were having a really bad time, near the bottom of the league and we, the players were being criticised every Sunday and Monday. That was it but the manager was getting it every day and he never once came in and said: 'You're the reason for this. ' He carried the burden himself.

BRIAN McCLAIR on Alex Ferguson.

It's pressure that makes the game beautiful.

ERIC CANTONA.

PROBLEMS

We were very disappointed we couldn't play on Saturday, because like United we had supporters coming from all over the country. There were two coming from London, one from Newcastle, one from Brighton.

ROCHDALE chairman David Kilpatrick after his side's 3rd round FA Cup tie against United was postponed.

When problems crop up I constantly preach patience and try to practice that virtue

MATT BUSBY.

We Scots have produced some of the world's great seafaring men, yet I doubt if any of them have suffered more ups and downs than I have.

WILLIE MORGAN.

This is the first thing I have got to live down, being regarded as some sort of shadow for Georgie Best. Even the landlady's son where I am in digs seemed a bit put out that I didn't perform wonders in my first trial match. People really do expect you to be something else because you grew up at Old Trafford.

FRANCIS BURNS, who played in the late 1960s and early 70s, after moving to Southampton.

To achieve happiness you sometimes have to go through the worst depths of despair.

ERIC CANTONA.

PROBLEMS

My mother always told me to look after the little one. I had to take him with me wherever I went and I moaned like hell about it. Later, when we played against each other in league football, I remember she was still telling me to lay off him. It didn't really matter because I could never catch him even then.

JACK CHARLTON.

He is accused of being arrogant, unable to cope with the pressure and a boozer. Sounds like he's got a chance to me.

GEORGE BEST on Paul Gascoigne.

We had problems with the wee feller, but I prefer to remember his genius.

MATT BUSBY on George Best.

Most of the things I've done are my own fault, so I can't feel guilty about them.

GEORGE BEST.

Mentally and physically I am a bloody wreck. Not eating. Not sleeping. Heavy drinking and staying out until four or five in the morning because I was frightened to go to my gold fish bowl of a home.

GEORGE BEST.

Every day there was a story in the papers about George Best - but most of the things we were reading were not about what he had done on the field, but about sleeping with three Miss Worlds or whatever. I cancelled the *Daily Mirror*, because I was sick to death of reading all their stories about George.

JACK CHARLTON.

Just as I wanted to outdo everyone when I played, I had to outdo everyone when we were on the town - always the last to go home.

GEORGE BEST.

Why does everybody hate us? I don't know and it doesn't bother me now.

ALEX FERGUSON.

I told them they were just a bunch of Fat Cats and that they were behaving like Billy Big Time.

ALEX FERGUSON to his players after a draw with Newcastle United

If someone says to me: 'Let him know that you are there', it does not mean that I should go up to my marker and say: 'Good afternoon, my name is Andrei Kanchelskis and I've just arrived from Kirovograd.' It means that you have to make your presence felt.

ANDREI KANCHELSKIS wrestling with the complexities of the English language after his arrival from Ukraine.

The year of the hamstring.

RON ATKINSON after a long run of injuries.

I was told by the surgeon that I could end up in a wheelchair at 35 or 40. That made up my mind for me.

NORMAN WHITESIDE who was forced to retire early because of injury.

There was a joke that Kevin [Moran] had more stitches in his head than in his suit.

RON ATKINSON.

If I hadn't come back to football I'd be in the gutter right now. I'm not kidding. Either that or I'd have been sweeping the streets.

GEORGE BEST.

PROBLEMS

Since 1969 his love life has been governed by nasty Uranus. It has been rather worse lately - that's been a lot of his trouble.

MARY ANDERSON, astrologist, on George Best in 1972.

I was able to stay in my natural environment and develop there as a respected member of the community. If I had been fifteen years old and pulled off the streets of Belfast onto the pitch at Old Trafford, I feel I would have ended up as George Best has.

BARRY JOHN, Welsh rugby great, on George Best.

RETIREMENT

Manchester United is a very special club. A club that I have searched for all my life but the time is right to move on.

ERIC CANTONA.

Be glad when all this presentation stuff is over. Nobody's going to put me in a home you know.

BOBBY CHARLTON after his last match for United.

I always felt I would recover from injury, but as time went on after the operation I knew I wouldn't be able to play again. It is a terrible thing to face. We all know that when we get into our 30s our playing days will terminate, but I was only 28. I didn't know what to do.

STEVE COPPELL who was forced to retire because of injury.

The only mistake Matt made in his career was to retire when he did.

BILL FOULKES.

There are things I could say about the situation here that I would regret later.

BOBBY CHARLTON as he retired.

He leaves with our best wishes and will always be welcome at Old Trafford.

ALEX FERGUSON after Eric Cantona announced his retirement.

RETIREMENT

It was a very sad day for this club when Eric decided to retire. He has been a fantastic player and is one of the most gifted players that I have ever had the pleasure of working with. Whenever United's fans discuss the club's greatest ever side you can be sure that Eric's name will be very high on the list.

ALEX FERGUSON.

I have played professional football for 13 years, which is a long time. I now wish to do other things. I have always planned to retire when I was at the top, and at Manchester United I have reached the pinnacle of my career.

ERIC CANTONA.

A footballer is like a precious flower that blossoms only for a short time, as one of our greatest contemporary philosophers might have said. In a dream, fame is sweeter than the tart flesh of apples to children. But sometimes the dream must come to an end and it is time to wake up. The poet must look out the window of the speeding train and know that his terminus is arriving. For every time there is a football season, there is a time to play and a time to go. Now it is the time to go and for the doctorates to be written.

THE INDEPENDENT newspaper on Eric Cantona's retirement.

I don't feel let down. This is the longest Eric has played for any club - a third of his career which is a measure of how he regarded United. There's absolutely no recriminations on my part. At £1 million we've had unbelievable value out of him, so we wish him well. We got six trophies for that money.

ALEX FERGUSON.

Eric Cantona has a unique talent and vision and has played a significant part in the development of the young players who have come through at Old Trafford. Four or five England footballers are all the better for that.

GRAHAM KELLY, Chief Executive of the Football Association.

It's breaking my heart. He's one of the world's greatest players and he'll be a tremendous loss.

UlRIKE JONSSON, television personality, on Canton's retirement.

Basically it's a case of: 'let's get on without him'. He has gone and it's not as if we're coming in here every day and saying: 'where's Eric? ' It makes you think what it would be like if you left yourself - nobody would give two hoots. But then this is a club that has lost a big player every season and it was the same when Bryan Robson left, Steve Bruce, Mark Hughes, Paul Ince and Andrei Kanchelskis - and now Eric. Life goes on without him.

GARY NEVILLE.

I do not understand how there can be a row with Manchester United. He loves the club and he loves the spectators. He was the master who gave the young players their voice. I am certain he will return to Old Trafford next month to say goodbye to the fans. Eric is not interested in money. Money is not what makes him tick. As you can see, he does not live in a castle and does not pursue a life of materialism. The heart rules his life. That is the most important thing to him. If someone says he is being greedy, it is false.

ELEANORE CANTONA, Eric's Mum.

With his enthusiasm I like to think he will stay in the game, although he is an intelligent lad.

RON ATKINSON on Steve Coppell who was forced to retire because of injury.

I think I've attained such a level of celebrity status that cinema can only lessen it.

ERIC CANTONA.

SELF IMAGE

It's bloody tough being a legend.

RON ATKINSON.

I'm the new kid on the block.

ROY KEANE after signing for United.

I'm a footballer first, not a pop star, which is what they seem to want.

RYAN GIGGS.

What I was asking for was not just about how I might see myself in the history of this club. It was how I might help this club make history.

ALEX FERGUSON after negotiating a new contract in 1996.

I'm a whole-hearted player and I can't sit back and spray 50-yard passes around, take the occasional free-kick and that's my night's work. If I don't get stuck in I usually have a bad game. Work-rate is a vital part of my game and I can't change.

ROY KEANE.

Sometimes I feel like a one-man zoo.

GEORGE BEST in 1973.

The public thinks I'm nuts. I probably am.

MICKEY THOMAS.

I'm a better ball player than George Best. George definitely had the edge over me in finishing but when it comes to beating people and creating chances for others, well, I could lose George at that.

WILLIE MORGAN.

I'm no angel and I've had a lot of trouble.

ROY KEANE.

No one will ever equal Sir Matt Busby's achievements and influence at Old Trafford, but I'd like to go down as someone who did nearly as much. I'll be happy if at the end of the day people say: ' Well there could only be one Sir Matt but T.D. came close to his standards and was the right man to follow on.'

TOMMY DOCHERTY.

I'm a lucky guy to be where I am today. Forget the National Lottery - I've really hit the jackpot here at Old Trafford.

STEVE BRUCE in 1995.

This is my one chance at making something of my life. It's all I've got. Without my career I have nothing.

DAVID BECKHAM.

I was just one of the players who got the ball for better players to play with.

TONY DUNNE.

I've no left foot, I'm not too good in the air and I'm not that fast. I've loads of weaknesses.

NORMAN WHITESIDE.

SELF IMAGE

My career may have ended at Goodison Park, but I'm a Red Devil through and through.

NORMAN WHITESIDE.

I've never been a unique talent. I've always been working, working my way to the top.

TEDDY SHERINGHAM.

After Munich I got a couple of England caps but to try and put myself into perspective, let me say that I was not fit to polish the boots of Duncan Edwards and Eddie Colman.

WILF McGUINNESS.

Today I would undoubtedly be good enough to play in the First Division because I can trap a ball and pass it.

EAMON DUNPHY, journalist and former United player, in 1991.

I could never have been anything else but a footballer. I'm crap at anything else. I suppose that without football, I'd just be a layabout. Ask my Mum.

RYAN GIGGS.

I think the Doc bought me just to make the other players laugh.

GORDON HILL.

My settee - it's a big lolloping casual sort of thing and it's not too fancy. That just about sums me up.

LEE SHARPE.

I don't think I'm blessed with any outstanding skills, but you can guarantee that I always try to do my best. Sometimes it's not good enough but sometimes it is.

STEVE BRUCE.

It would be brilliant to be as big as Gazza. I would love to be that big.

DAVID BECKHAM.

Freedom of expression brings genius, brings euphoria, brings fire. I play with passion and fire. I have to accept that sometimes this fire does harm. I harm myself. I am aware of it. I harm others.

ERIC CANTONA.

You need a particular talent only to want to please. I don't have this talent.

ERIC CANTONA.

I'm an ordinary fellow. I never know what is expected of me when I'm introduced to people. If I talked a lot about myself, I'd be called bigheaded, so I say nothing. But whatever I did or said, there'd be some people who would find it wrong.

BOBBY CHARLTON.

I don't really class myself as a footballer. I call myself an entertainer.

GEORGE BEST.

Was I the fifth Beatle? Not really. What I think they meant was that I wasn't your average don't do anything until Saturday footballer.

GEORGE BEST.

They say the first thing that goes when you are getting older is your pace, but I never had much of that anyway.

MARK HUGHES.

Beneath this granite exterior beats a heart of stone.

MARTIN BUCHAN.

SELF IMAGE

I still have to pinch myself when I look around Old Trafford these days and feel the expectation of greatness and realise I am part of that legend.

PAUL INCE.

You can say I'm replacing Eric [Cantona], but I don't see it that way. It's a pressure in itself joining the club so I'm not getting involved in talking about succeeding Eric.

TEDDY SHERINGHAM.

Footballers are no different to a milkman or a dustman. We're just in the limelight and get paid a lot of money.

DAVID BECKHAM.

Just as I can bring happiness to people with my spontaneity, my instinctiveness, so there are always going to be dark shadows, black stains.

ERIC CANTONA.

I would not change anything, nothing at all. I am not always pleased with myself but that's the way I am.

ERIC CANTONA.

I'm not a caterer, I'm not really a businessman. I'm a footballer. Everyone should try to do the thing he does well. The thing I do well is football

GEORGE BEST.

I'm not a sex symbol, I'm a footballer.

GARY BAILEY.

THE SHEEPSKIN JACKETS

I have never joined in the popular game of belittling football club directors simply because they are football directors. I have always said, look at the top when analysing clubs who have lasting success, and there you will find the original cause of the happy effect.

MATT BUSBY.

I hate what has been going on. All the newspaper headlines, the speculation, the ugly rumours. United has been used as a political football which has been kicked around and it looks as if it might burst.

BOBBY CHARLTON on the controversy surrounding Michael Knighton's attempt to buy United.

It falls on my shoulders, but I'll say until my dying day that no chairman ever won a match.

MARTIN EDWARDS, United's Chief Executive.

Talking to [Michael] Knighton is rather like talking to Basil Fawlty: don't mention the war, But no matter what you planned to say you end up talking about Manchester United.

SIMON BARNES, writer, in 1997.

I'm drunk on adrenalin.

MICHAEL KNIGHTON after becoming a Director of United.

I was jubilant. I'd fulfilled my childhood dream. I was at the greatest club in the world and I was chairman-elect. I wanted to let the Stretford End know that I was one of them. Look at the photos; they're all smiling and so am I.

MICHAEL KNIGHTON explaining his cavorting in front of goal at Old Trafford after he became Director of the club.

It was [Robert] Maxwell who turned it. He had 22 million readers and he'd tried and failed to buy the club twice. He went for the windpipe like a Rottweiler.

MICHAEL KNIGHTON explaining his departure from the club.

My signature is on some of the most important contracts ever signed by Manchester United. We won six trophies. I gave them the kick up the arse that they desperately needed, even if that makes me sound like an arrogant little shit. I'm proud of what happened at Old Trafford since I became involved. I don't take credit, but I was the catalyst.

MICHAEL KNIGHTON.

Anybody who swears allegiance to United must share the same sense of dismay at what has happened and what is still going on - for me, it's almost a sense of revulsion. No more shabby deals.

PAT CRERAND on the ownership row in 1989.

That great club is slowly being destroyed. And I blame one family for the ruin. The Edwards family. The master butchers of Manchester.

HARRY GREGG as he left United.

We're not into minority sports.

BARRY HEARN, snooker and boxing manager, denying rumours that he was going to bid for United.

VERBALS

You know Dennis Wise. He could start a fight in an empty room.

ALEX FERGUSON.

They've obviously never been to a Glasgow wedding.

ALEX FERGUSON declaring no worries about the possible hostile atmosphere at United's clash with Galatasara in Turkey.

He has no experience of English football - he's come from Japan - and now he is telling everyone how to organise our football. Unless you have been in the situation and have the experience, then he should keep his mouth shut - firmly shut.

ALEX FERGUSON on Arsene Wenger and the fixture backlog dispute at the end of the 1997 season.

Nobby Stiles a dirty player? No, he's never hurt anyone. Mind you, he's frightened a few.

MATT BUSBY.

The provocation and intimidation at Anfield is incredible. I can understand why clubs come away from here choking on their own vomit and biting their tongues knowing they have been done by the referee. When you lose it sounds like sour grapes, but we got a result and I'm saying it.

ALEX FERGUSON after a 3-3 draw with Liverpool.

I get stick everywhere. Makes me feel at home.

ROY KEANE.

Don't look round when you come down the tunnel at Burnden Park on Saturday because I'm going to bury a hatchet in your head.

LETTER WRITTEN to Nobby Stiles before a match at Bolton.

Their tactics began to resemble a commando raid: knock out the main installations - which meant the key players - then get on with the job.

DENIS LAW on the Leeds United team in the 1960s and 70s.

The BBC are dying for us to lose. Everyone is from Liverpool with a supporter's badge.

ALEX FERGUSON.

Do they hate us? You take a corner kick at Elland Road and you've got 15,000 horrible skinheads in their end yelling murder at you.

RYAN GIGGS.

All I know is that I'll never be able to achieve what Tommy [Docherty] did and that is take Aston Villa into the Third Division, and better than that, take Manchester United into the Second Division.

RON ATKINSON.

If Tommy Docherty says good morning to you you'd better check the weather outside.

GEORGE BEST.

Hard men? Well, there was that picture of Vinnie Jones holding Gazza's wotsits. In my day we called someone who did that a poof.

GEORGE BEST.

When I get kicked I'm supposed to count to ten and then walk away. I can't. If a player deliberately kicks me, I'll kick him back.

DENIS LAW.

Being face to face with Alex Ferguson can be an unnerving experience. It can be the same feeling you might get if you were asked to go 12 rounds with Lennox Lewis.

ANDREI KANCHELSKIS.

At Anfield things tend to be a bit more basic. They throw 50p pieces at me, yelling abuse. I have my own way of dealing with that. I put the ball down, take one step, kick it and then run off to the safety of the penalty area, where I've only got Neil Ruddock to worry about.

RYAN GIGGS.

Every team had a hard man. We had Nobby Stiles, Chelsea had Chopper, Arsenal had Peter Storey, Liverpool had Tommy Smith. Leeds had 11 of them.

GEORGE BEST.

It would probably take an Act of Parliament, instigated by the new soccer task force of Tony Banks and David Mellor, to stop [Alex] Ferguson's perpetual moaning.

HARRY HARRIS, journalist.

Best has given footballers a bad name and I saw it as my job to repair their reputation. It took a long time and a lot of hard work, but I like to think I helped.

KEVIN KEEGAN.

He's not fit to lace my boots as a player.

GEORGE BEST on Kevin Keegan.

VERBALS

Keegan is not fit to lace George Best's drinks.

JOHN ROBERTS, journalist.

As an enemy, Doc was vicious, vindictive and callous.

PAT CRERAND.

I get to my feet when Chelsea fans sing: ' Stand Up If You Hate Man United. '

KEN BATES, Chairman of Chelsea.

Roy Keane thinks he's a hard man. Lock him up in a cell with another con, a knife each and no clothes on. Then we'll see how hard he is.

' MAD ' FRANKIE FRASER, former criminal.

After a reserve game at Forfar, he was shouting and wagging his finger at one of the boys. In his anger he kicked the laundry basket and these pants flew through the air and landed on another guy's head like a hat. He didn't move. Just sat there rigid. Fergie didn't even notice until he had finished raging. Then he looked up at the boy and said 'And you can take those f****** pants off your head. What the hell do you think you're playing at?'

MARK McGEE recalling an incident when he was one of Alex Ferguson's players at Aberdeen.

I don't really like playing against the clever ones like Gascoigne. I prefer someone like Whiteside, where you can get stuck in, get a bit back and have a good laugh about it.

VINNIE JONES.

If you're not careful I'll buy Maine Road and use it as our training ground.

TOMMY DOCHERTY to Manchester City Chairman Peter Swales.

Since I was not completely dead and since I even resurrected, they have done everything they could to make sure I died a second time. We'll see who dies in the end.

ERIC CANTONA after being left out of the French squad for Euro '96.

The French team has lived and won without him. This is a team that plays well, that feels good together.

AIME JACQUET, French coach.

Aime Jacquet has once again given Cantona his favourite role, that of martyr. The decision will embellish the legend of the cursed player, crucified by others when he does not indulge in self destruction.

L'Equipe newspaper.

It's as if I were on the roof of a building in New York, looking down, and seeing a lot of small people passing by.

ERIC CANTONA on the French football authorities.

I once asked Bobby Charlton the best way to get to United's training ground and I'm still waiting for the answer.

TED MacDOUGALL.

He wears No. 10. I thought it was his position but it turns out to be his IQ.

GEORGE BEST on Paul Gascoigne.

I couldn't get up and mingle even if I wanted to. There's always someone who wants to start a fight. Every time I go to the gents a couple of friends have to come along as well for protection.

GEORGE BEST

George thought he was the James Bond of soccer. He had everything he wanted and he pleased himself. He had money, girls and tremendous publicity. He lived from day to day. Until right at the end he got away with it when he missed training or ran away. So he didn't care. People made excuses for him; he didn't even have to bother to do it himself.

People talked about pressures and depressions. It was rubbish. He just hadn't any responsibilities, nothing to worry about at all. All kinds of people covered up for him, even the Press, and he was lucky to get away with it for so long.

WILLIE MORGAN.

There are plenty of reasons why he won't last and the main one, sad to say, is he's just not good enough

GEORGE BEST on Paul Gascoigne.

I don't want to end up like him.

GASCOIGNE on Best.

We were going to Portugal for our holiday, but now it looks like Bermuda. That may be just far enough away to steer clear of George Best and all his problems.

BOBBY CHARLTON.

I used to hit people over the head with my handbag if they shouted names like 'dirty Jones' when Mark committed a foul or if they threw other abuse at him when he made a mistake.

JUNE JONES, widow of Mark Jones.

He can't run, he can't tackle and he can't head a ball. The only time he goes forward is to toss the coin.

TOMMY DOCHERTY on Ray Wilkins.

When Geoff Thomas traps the ball it goes as far as I used to be able to kick it.

GEORGE BEST.

Nobby Stiles is a dangerous marker, tenacious and sometimes brutal. He takes recourse to anything to contain his man. Very badly intentioned. A bad sportsman.

OTTO GLORIA, Benfica coach.

If I wasn't like that I wouldn't be able to play because that's my way of concentrating. You should see Pally and Bruce's faces, they're worse. For them and for me it's just an expression that we're in the game.

PETER SCHMEICHEL, on his screaming and shouting.

Quite honestly, if England played in my back garden I'd close the curtains.

GEORGE BEST in 1970.

I've not been feeling too good and the medicine man said 'get away from football. '

TOMMY DOCHERTY explaining to the Manchester City chairman why he had gone to Maine Road.

The present United side would have beaten the Sixties team 10-0.

PETER SCHMEICHEL.

Peter's got a fair point. After all, we're all over 50 now.

NOBBY STILES.

I used to say he was a great asset to television because they didn't need slow motion when he was on the ball.

DENIS LAW on Pat Crerand.

VERBALS

He could start an argument in an empty house.

JIMMY NICHOLL on Tommy Docherty.

Stiles. The Assassin of Madrid.

SPANISH NEWSPAPER headline after United beat Real Madrid in the semi-final of the 1968 European Cup.

Then we were laughing and I was somehow happy I'd been hit with the bottle. If we had lost they would have thrown flowers at me.

NOBBY STILES who was struck by a bottle after the same game.

Come back here, you scumbag. You ratbag, you dirty bastard.

ALEX FERGUSON to Feyenoord defender Paul Bosvelt after his foul on Dennis Irwin.

You have to retain a sense of normality even if you can't have a normal life. If you bump into somebody whose talking rubbish you have to bite your lip. If you're a normal guy and somebody is really irritating, you can bop them, have a quick scuffle, then disappear. You'd probably get away with it. But no matter how much you've been provoked, if you are caught arguing in a pub, it's the footballer who'll always get the blame.

BRIAN McCLAIR.

WINNING

Was I surprised by the scoreline? Well I'll say: ' yes ' to be polite.

ERIC CANTONA after United beat Newcastle 4-0 in the 1996 Charity Shield.

We only came here by invitation because Manchester United had won everything. Now I wish they had invited somebody else.

KEVIN KEEGAN after the same match.

The ref should blow his whistle. It's like watching a fatally wounded animal.

ALAN GREEN, radio commentator, during the same match.

I can't think of anything that can be better than today's double.

ALEX FERGUSON after United won the Double Double.

I'm pleased for everybody from Manchester United - the players, the fans, the staff and my man Ned [his bodyguard]. Today I feel half English, half French and half Irish.

ERIC CANTONA after scoring the winner in the 1996 F.A. Cup Final and assuring United of the Double Double.

They've won the title without being fantastic. Nobody else has been good enough to take advantage.

HARRY REDKNAPP, West Ham boss, after United won the title in 1997.

That's the least they deserve, a little bit of recognition for their achievements.

KENNY DALGLISH who got his Newcastle United players to form a guard of honour for Manchester United as they took the field following their fourth title win in five years.

We stand on our own. We have won this without the help of the Premiership. It is not a chip on my shoulder, just a recognition that we have done it on our own. There is a terrible amount of jealousy towards Manchester United. I do not know why.

ALEX FERGUSON after winning the Premiership in 1997.

The first thing is to congratulate them even though it sticks in your throat.

ROY EVANS, Liverpool boss, on the same event.

They are the flagship side that we've all got to try and beat. Good luck to Alex, no doubt he'll be voted Manager of the Year again, lucky bastard.

JOE KINNEAR, Wimbledon boss, after United won the Premier League in 1997.

You strive all your life to get a feeling like tonight.

ALEX FERGUSON after United won the Premier League in 1993.

Alex has had to wait seven years for this but I've been waiting for 26.

MARTIN EDWARDS, Chief Executive after United won the title in 1993.

There has been a lot of talk about getting married but if Manchester United win the championship I definitely will.

GEORGE BEST.

I am over the moon, as they say these days, and I mean that - the English League is still the hardest in the world to win. This team has exciting qualities and character after losing its way a third through the season.

MATT BUSBY after United won the championship in 1993.

It has been hard work to win the Premier League but it has all paid off. This is a difficult club to manage. There's a lot of pressure involved in the job. The standards are high here. We've set our own standards now with this triumph and we mustn't let those standards drop.

ALEX FERGUSON after United won the Premiership in 1993

I think he's on the verge of setting up what we'll look back on and call the Fergie Dynasty to match the Busby Dynasty.

WILF McGUINNESS after United won the premiership in 1993.

There are still some poignant memories. Of going to the all-night banquet at the Russell Hotel and seeing Duncan Edwards' parents, and Eddie Colman's parents. All the parents of the Munich victims were invited. I didn't know what to say to them and there were a lot of tears. It was very sad. I kept thinking if he had been alive, Duncan would have been playing instead of me.

PAT CRERAND recalling the night United won the European Cup.

At the end I felt six foot-two tall. Afterwards I took my wife to Danny LaRue's club and had a whale of a time.

NOBBY STILES recalling the same event.

I told them they were throwing the game away. They were giving the ball away and hitting it anywhere instead of using it. I said they must hold it and start to play football again.

MATT BUSBY to his players during the break before extra time in the European Cup Final.

Before the eyes of millions, they were thrown into the Wembley arena against a Leicester team that has been one of the most feared forces in football this year And they returned in triumph to release the joy of 300,000 people in an outburst of emotion that has not been seen since the dramatic night when the new Babes stepped out of Munich

THE MANCHESTER EVENING NEWS after United won the 1963 Cup Final.

If the game had had another ten minutes to go, we would have lost. We were on top but when they scored, it knocked the heart out of us. We were tired. It was like the World Cup final all over again.

NOBBY STILES on the European Cup Final.

I always find it frustrating when my goal is shown on TV because you only see me taking the ball around the keeper. Alex had cleared the ball, David flicked it on and I stuck it through the centre-half's legs. I was more chuffed with that than anything. The keeper made my mind up for me by coming out quite quickly, so I took the ball round him. I thought about walking it in, or stopping it on the line and kneeling down to head it in, but finally thought better of it.

GEORGE BEST on his goal in the European Cup Final.

I have chased and chased this European Cup with many disappointments, but here it is at last. I am the proudest man in England tonight.

MATT BUSBY after winning the European Cup.

The one against Leicester City was the greatest academic final perhaps of all time.

MATT BUSBY on the 1963 F.A. Cup Final.

Are you listening, Big Fat Ron?

UNITED FANS as they celebrated winning the Premiership in 1993.

Winning isn't everything. There should be no conceit in victory and no despair in defeat.

MATT BUSBY.

Sir Matt wandered round with this beatific look on his face for days afterwards.

GEORGE BEST after United finally won the European Cup.

We were on the 18th. green and a man I had never met before walked over the hill and said: 'Excuse me, Mr.Ferguson, you are the champions. Oldham have just beaten Villa. '

HOW ALEX FERGUSON learned that United had won the title in 1993 for the first time in 26 years.

I want to win and I take more satisfaction from what I have achieved here than at Aberdeen. The pressures are greater here.

ALEX FERGUSON.

Success hasn't changed me and I won't allow it to. It hasn't changed Sir Matt Busby or Bobby Charlton.

ALEX FERGUSON.

It was like something from Roy of the Rovers.

GEORGE BEST on winning the European Cup in 1968.

The success he has had hasn't affected him - but the success he hasn't had has left a mark. He badly wants to win the European Cup, not for himself but for Manchester United. Personally, I think he deserves it for himself.

JOE MERCER on Matt Busby before United won the European Cup.

All I wanted to do afterwards was to get away to some pub where I could sit quietly in a corner and drink some beer.

TONY DUNNE recalling the night United won the European Cup.

WINNING

It's not your achievements that matter. Winning a trophy last year is good for a while but then you have to go and meet the next challenge because that's your life.

ALEX FERGUSON.

I will always remain the hungriest person at Old Trafford. If I allow that to slip, then the club has no chance. That's why I won't get carried away by having won the Double for the second time.

ALEX FERGUSON.

When Kevin Moran got sent off and Norman Whiteside got the winner, that was the first time I heard United fans sing ' Always look on the Whiteside of life ' which was superb.

TERRY CHRISTIAN, television personality.

Hopefully we can use this as a platform. Having experienced this tonight you need it all the time now, it becomes a drug.

ALEX FERGUSON after United won the European Cup Winners' Cup in 1991.

Winning things is great business. Hey, when you've got a great team, all of a sudden people don't complain if the rolls in the hospitality restaurant are stale.

DANNY McGREGOR, United's Commercial Manager.

Like Satchmo says, it's a wonderful world.

MATT BUSBY as he arrived back in Manchester after United's European Cup semi-final victory over Real Madrid in 1968.

How appropriate that there should be 39 steps for Buchan to climb to receive the Cup.

JOHN MOTSON, referring to the novel by John Buchan, The Thirty Nine Strpes as Martin Buchan climbed the 39 steps at Wembley Stadium to collect the FA Cup in 1977.

Ferguson may be in charge only three years, for example, but as far as United fans are concerned, it's his fault that it's 23 years since they won the League Championship.

KEVIN MORAN.

I want to see the team winning and playing attractively. Which comes first ? It must be winning.

DAVE SEXTON on his appointment as manager.

It's just too memorable for words.

BOBBY CHARLTON after United won the Premiership in 1993.

You get greedier every season and want to win everything. Despite winning the League title last year and getting to the semi-final of the European Cup, I didn't want to watch the FA Cup Final because I was jealous.

ROY KEANE.

It has done my players a world of good to be associated with such a team on the same pitch. But I wish they had suspended Best for five weeks !

DAVE BOWEN, the Northampton manager, after losing 6-0 to United in the Cup. George Best scored six on his return from a four week's suspension.

Manchester United deserve the trophy every year for having to live and play here.

A YEOVIL SUPPORTER after his team lost 8-0 to United at Old Trafford in the 1949 FA Cup.

Some people change with success. Some always want to go to Glasgow on holiday. Some want to go to France.

ALEX FERGUSON.

We planned to contain them. But George must have had cotton wool in his ears when we decided our tactics. Within the first quarter of an hour he had beaten them on his own with two goals and another made for Connelly. It was fantastic and I was angry with him. Well, almost.

MATT BUSBY on Best after United's 5-1 defeat of Benfica in 1966.

You must eat, sleep and dream football to reach the top.

BILL FOULKES.

Arguably the greatest cup win any side will ever have at Wembley.

RON ATKINSON after United won the 1985 F.A. Cup final during which Kevin Moran was sent off.

WOMEN

If you want the secret of my success with women, then don't smoke, don't take drugs and don't be too particular.

GEORGE BEST.

I would like the girl I marry to be a virgin. It used to be one of the most important things I used to think about. Finding a girl who was a virgin. But it's almost impossible for it to work. In fact it's almost impossible to find a girl who's a virgin. My ideas must be changing though 'cos I don't feel as strongly about it as I used to. And if I did find a girl who was a virgin I probably wouldn't like her anyway.

GEORGE BEST.

Only one person tells me what to do - my wife Jean.

MATT BUSBY.

Once I started playing football I realised I was in the perfect position for pulling birds. I had the limelight, the publicity, the money. Where could I go wrong?

GEORGE BEST.

I wouldn't kiss any girl if she smoked too much.

GEORGE BEST.

They say I've slept with seven Miss Worlds. I didn't. It was only four. I didn't turn up for the other three.

GEORGE BEST.

What would you do if you weren't a footballer ?

Manage the Miss World contest. I might get the four birds I missed.

GEORGE BEST at a question and answer session.

I have often wondered and perhaps you'll tell me, George. Exactly how big is your willy ?

QUESTION from a girl to George Best during a personal appearance.

It's like George Best once said to me: 'When you've had the last three Miss Worlds, then you can start talking.'

MAURICE JOHNSTON.

Mary Stavin is the only woman to whom I was almost always faithful.

GEORGE BEST.

There was an earthquake when I gave birth. I witnessed bombing, shooting, explosions and death at first hand. After that I can assure you that George Best is pretty easy to cope with.

MARY SHATILA, George Best's girlfriend.

Once you get the taste of George Best you never want to taste another thing.

ANGIE BEST in 1979.

He's one of the most intelligent, considerate and generous of men. I still love him, but there are problems better solved on his own.

MARY STAVIN as she left George Best.

You leave Giggsy alone. He's been playing crap since he met you.

FAN to Ryan Giggs's then girlfriend, Dani Behr.

SPEAK OF THE DEVILS

It is irrelevant whether Giggs dates Dani Behr or Yogi Bear - provided he lights up our Saturday.

HENRY WINTER, journalist.

We've got matching dogs, matching watches, similar wardrobes, matching Jags. I like all that. I know it's really tacky but it makes me laugh.

POSH SPICE.

YOUTH

The first time I entered the dressing room to meet the other players I wondered if I was in the right place. There were so many
other youngsters that it seemed like being back at school.

DUNCAN EDWARDS.

I was scared of the youth team coach when I got there. To be honest, though, when you first arrive at Man United you're scared of
just about everything.

GARY NEVILLE.

I gave up a lot when I was younger. Going out with the lads,
going to parties and discos, leaving my family to come up to
Manchester. It was what I wanted though, so I made my choices.

DAVID BECKHAM.

My young life revolved around playing football. There was no
television then and people lived by their radio sets. All the kids
did was play football in the streets. You kicked a ball against the
wall all the way to school, then you had a game when you got
there. At mid morning break you had another game and you
kicked a ball all the way home at lunchtime, and so it went on.

DENIS LAW.

Where I was brought up, you had to be able to run or fight and
you know about my running.

PAT CRERAND.

SPEAK OF THE DEVILS

The greatest, most fulfilling joy a manager can have is that of seeing a young boy arrive unknown, step on the field of play and then realise you have seen a great star make his debut.

MATT BUSBY.

I couldn't wear glasses to play in a proper match of course, so I developed a unique system for coping with the problem. I learned to play football with one eye closed. I kept my glasses on as long as I could, while I put on my jersey and socks and boots, but when the moment came to go on the pitch and the glasses had to come off, I used to close my right eye and keep it closed for the whole of the match. I learned to play through an entire game using only one eye and I went on doing this for years.

DENIS LAW who suffered from a squint as a youth.

In those days when I was a kid the only thing I shared my bed with was a football. I used to take the ball to bed with me. I know it sounds daft but I used to love the feel of it. I used to hold it, look at it and think: ' One day you'll do everything I tell you. '

GEORGE BEST.

I had four teenagers in Aberdeen's 1983 European Cup-Winners' Cup side and none of them are still playing today. I have to ask myself: 'Should I have rested them?' I don't want to make the same mistake.

ALEX FERGUSON.

If they are good enough, they are old enough

MATT BUSBY.

It's very flattering when you're 14 and Alex Ferguson comes in for you. You tend to think: yeah.

RYAN GIGGS.

People say that it was a poor upbringing. I don't know what they mean. It was tough but it wasn't bloody poor. We maybe didn't have a television. We didn't have a car. We didn't even have a phone. But I thought I had everything and I did. I had football.

ALEX FERGUSON.

We played in the streets mainly, or in the park. Whoever had a ball and got there first would start a game and more boys and men came and joined in until it was 20 or 30 a side. We kept it going all day long. Lunch was the only thing that would make me stop and even the men would only leave to have a drink. It wasn't just youngsters - it was all ages.

BOBBY CHARLTON.

People won't believe me when I tell them I played the church organ down in the Rhondda when I was 15. I can best forget football playing Beethoven, Bach and the other great composers on the organ and piano. I like to read too - Mark Twain and Chesterton. You can learn a lot from those fellows.

JIMMY MURPHY in 1962.

It's nonsense to argue that a kid gets a better chance over there (Manchester City). If a father is choosing an apprenticeship for his son, he's always going to take Rolls Royce over the local engineering shop.

ALEX FERGUSON.

I don't want to butter you up, Missus, but your boy will play for England before he's 21.

JOE ARMSTRONG, United scout, to Bobby Charlton's Mum in 1953.

I was a skinhead in a duffle coat and Doc Martens with my football boots in a plastic bag tucked under my arm.

HOW NORMAN WHITESIDE dressed when he travelled over to Old Trafford as a youth.

I was brought up with many of them. They were going to prison,
I was going to the World Cup.

NORMAN WHITESIDE.

Her aunt owned a cake shop in Manchester and we went to bed
for the first time in the flat above the store. Then we rushed
downstairs again and helped ourselves to cakes

GEORGE BEST on an early fling.

I used to wait for my father to come back from the match on a
Saturday and he would always give me the programme. Even as a
child United was my team.

MARTIN EDWARDS.

He was so small it was like picking up a baby. But that didn't stop
him scoring eight goals in one game, every one with his head.

ONE OF Paul Scholes' teachers.

One of the biggest thrills of my life was when I got my first United
blazer to go on a youth tour to Ireland. I stopped people to see
how they thought it looked on me

ALBERT SCANLON.

I'm one of the few people in this world who've been across the
pitch at Old Trafford on my hands and knees getting weeds out
with a little dibber and a bucket. They used to put string lanes
about a yard wide across the pitch and about four or five of us
used to have to do the weeding. Old Scott Duncan was the manager then and he used to come behind you and if you missed a
weed he used to say: 'Hey, lad, come on, there's one here.'

STAN PEARSON.

Boy Best Flashes in Red Attack.

**MANCHESTER EVENING NEWS' headline after George Best's
debut for Manchester United against West Brom.**

He was one of my heroes. I used to sit on my Dad's shoulders and watch him.....I used to call him Sir Allenby de Trafford.... he was a mighty centre-half.

NOBBY STILES on Allenby Chilton.

The kids are all right.

ALEX FERGUSON.

A young man has a right to rebel.

ERIC CANTONA.

I wish I never had to grow up.

ERIC CANTONA.

He became a cult of youth, a new folk hero, a living James Dean who was a rebel with a cause.

GEOFFREY GREEN, journalist, on George Best.

I live in hope that one day I'll go along to a youth match, as in 1963, watch an unknown kid for five minutes and find myself asking: 'My God - who is that ?'

PAT CRERAND on the search for another George Best.

Looking back I feel guilty. George Best was a youngster when he came into a great side and I don't think we senior players took enough interest in him. Older players influenced me a great deal when I was young, but we failed to influence George Best.

BILL FOULKES.

In addition to the letters, I have a fan club of 900, a personal secretary, two spare-time assistants, a literary agent, an accountant, a teenager's boutique, two more shops on the way, a white 3.4 Jag convertible with radio, tape-recorders and dozens of girlfriends.

GEORGE BEST.

They should show the kids films of his matches. They'd learn more from five minutes of George than they would from five years of coaching videos.

PAT JENNINGS on George Best
.

In February 1961 he took a 15-year-old Belfast boy on to his playing staff, and although he didn't know it at the time, by doing so he achieved his ambition and fulfilled his dream. The boy's name was George Best and from the moment he signed for United nothing was the same again, not for Sir Matt, nor the club, and most certainly not for George Best.

MICHAEL PARKINSON, writer and broadcaster.

I am going to protect Ryan all I can. I have got to be honest and say George [Best] is the role model of what to avoid with our talented kids. I use George's case as an example when I speak to parents of young footballers. Everybody wanted a piece of George. This club is a refuge for Ryan. He can come and be sheltered by us. When the time comes and he can handle it, then we won't stand in his way.

ALEX FERGUSON.

I was almost in tears watching him perform.

ALAN SMITH, who used to run Greater Manchester County Schools under-15 team, on Ryan Giggs.

One spotty virgin, there's only one spotty virgin.

UNITED supporters to Ryan Giggs during his early days in the first team.

You don't argue with the boss. But he's kind. He treats you like his son and you can talk to him.

DAVID BECKHAM.

He was never a kid, always a man.

RON ATKINSON on Norman Whiteside.

I'm not a discoverer of players. There can be no discovery without revelation.

BOB BISHOP, United's Northern Ireland scout.

I wanted to be an architect. What are you laughing for? I really did.

DENIS LAW.

In my career everything has come so fast it frightens me.

DAVID BECKHAM.

I suppose it was instinct really. The difference between a good player and a great player is that great players can read the game. That's something you cannot teach a guy - he either has it or he hasn't and if he has he's half-way there. But you can't teach him to think.

BILLY BEHAN, scout.

I was very impressed with young Giggs when I saw him play for United at Chelsea. He looks like a great prospect.

JOHN MAJOR, MP.

One of the secret's of Manchester United's success is that nearly all of us grew up together as boy footballers. We were knitted into a football family.

ROGER BYRNE.

I have found a genius.

BOB BISHOP, United's Northern Ireland scout, to Matt Busby about George Best.

While you could say we've had a great ten years, there's also been a preparation for the next ten years. Because of youth we're designed to be one step ahead.

ALEX FERGUSON.

I was always a dead-keen Red, and if you came from our area there was no such thing as a soccer connoisseur. None of this liberal nonsense of hoping both sides did well.

NOBBY STILES.

Always be ready and willing to listen to your elders, and keep yourself fit at all times.

BOBBY CHARLTON.

I really wanted to accept because I'd always loved the game. But I stopped to assess it and asked myself what's the length of a footballer's career?

SEAN CONNERY who turned down Matt Busby's offer to join United.

We used the arches of a warehouse for goals; the street lights used to light the place up, and we would play until all hours.

BRIAN KIDD.

I think Manchester United is the greatest club in the world, Mr. Busby. I'd give anything to play for your team.

DUNCAN EDWARDS.

He was of nice disposition and sound character. He was a born footballer. He would come to school with a tennis ball in his pocket and kick it about the asphalt playground. I thought then that if he could control a tennis ball like he did he might one day play at Wembley. He was a good, quiet lad, with no bounce about him.

ALDERMAN J S MARLOW, then Mayor of Dudley, after the death of Duncan Edwards.

The 1958 World Cup series brought glory to Brazil and a 17-year-old wonder man named Pele. But I often wonder, would it have been a different story for Brazil, and especially for Pele, had he been playing against our superstar Duncan Edwards.

FRANK TAYLOR, journalist, who survived the Munich disaster.

There is a playing field near my lodgings in Stretford and I go out there and watch the school matches. Do you know - I think I would rather watch them than any other kind of football. They give it everything. Who ever heard of a kid not trying on the football field?

DUNCAN EDWARDS.

Duncan Edwards was a man in football but still a boy at heart. His ability was good enough for England but his potential was good enough for Heaven.

JACKIE BLANCHFLOWER.

This big lad came up to me at the start of the game and said: 'Reputations mean nothing to me and if you come near me I'll kick you over the stand. ' And that's just what he tried to do as soon as I got the ball. United beat us 5-2 in that game. What a team they had - and what a player that big lad Duncan [Edwards] was. He was a nice lad too for all his size and power. After the game he came up to me and said: 'It was a pleasure playing against you. '

JACKIE MILBURN.

When I used to hear Muhammad Ali proclaim to the world that he was the greatest, I used to smile. You see, the greatest of them all was an English footballer named Duncan Edwards.

JIMMY MURPHY.

Nicky Butt used to clean my boots - I'm the only black person to have a white shoeshine boy.

PAUL PARKER.

TAKING EACH QUOTE
AS IT COMES

Tell me, Mr.Best - where did it all go wrong?

A PORTER who arrived in Best's hotel suite to deliver champagne where he saw £15,000 spread out on the bed and half-naked Miss World, Mary Stavin prancing about the room.

I saw a sign saying 'Drink Canada Dry.'

GEORGE BEST explaining why he went to America.

I'd have to be superman to do some of the things I'm supposed to have done. I've been in six different places at six different times.

GEORGE BEST.

Sometimes I think it would be nice to get married and settle down, but there's a long time for that, isn't there?

GEORGE BEST.

The only thing I have in common with George Best is that we came from the same place, play for the same club and were discovered by the same man.

NORMAN WHITESIDE.

He is as brave as a VC winner.

BOBBY CHARLTON on George Best.

TAKING EACH QUOTE AS IT COMES

My only reaction upon hearing that George Best had been named Footballer of the Year by claiming 60 per cent of the vote was to ask my informant: 'Who on earth did the remaining 40 per cent vote for? '

MICHAEL PARKINSON after Best became Footballer of the Year in 1968.

If George Best were an Englishman we would keep the World Cup for the next ten years.

BOBBY CHARLTON.

People say he wasted his career. Nonsense, he was hunted down by defenders for 11 full seasons, starting at 17. He paid his dues all right.

DAVID MEEK, journalist, on George Best.

The man who can understand George is on a winner.

STEVE FULLAWAY, son of George Best's landlady.

How do you rate Jimmy Greaves?

The only man who could drink more than me.

GEORGE BEST during a question and answer sessioN.

Really he's still the same little boy lost that he was when he first came to Manchester.

MRS. FULLAWAY, George Best's former landlady in Manchester.

He is a son of instinct rather than logic.

GEOFFREY GREEN, journalist, on George Best.

People say the English are arrogant. I say they have reason.

ERIC CANTONA.

In 1969 I gave up drinking and sex. It was the worst bloody 20 minutes of my life.

GEORGE BEST.

He should have been captain and more respected as a footballer, because he's an intelligent lad, not the fool that people take him for.

EAMON DUNPHY on George Best.

It's the collective part of the team that is important. If I'd wanted to draw attention to myself I'd have played singles tennis or chosen a nice lady for mixed doubles.

ERIC CANTONA.

The only thing I don't understand about the English is why they are so interested in the weather. One day it's light grey, the next it's dark grey.

ERIC CANTONA.

Oh, come on, ref. Even I could see that.

A BLIND UNITED FAN listening to the radio commentary at Old Trafford.

Can anybody tell me why they give referees a watch? It's certainly not to keep the time. I think it was a Mickey Mouse one.

ALEX FERGUSON unhappy at referee Graham Poll's reluctance to add more than three minutes injury time in the clash with Everton.

I have to hand it to Manchester United. They have the best players-and the best referees.

SAM HAMMAM, owner of Wimbledon.

1966 was a great year for English football. Eric was born

NIKE advertising poster.

Wherever I've gone, it's my body, my head and my eyes which have played.

ERIC CANTONA

Genius is about digging yourself out of this big hole which you find yourself in, or in which others have put you. That's genius. Genius is not about complaining.

ERIC CANTONA.

When seagulls follow the trawler, it is because they think that sardines will be thrown into the sea.

ERIC CANTONA.

If a Frenchman goes on about seagulls, trawlers and sardines, he's called a philosopher. I'd be called a short Scottish bum talking rubbish.

GORDON STRACHAN.

The only relaxation I wanted from football was to play more football and that, I feel sure, is the only way to learn this, the greatest game in the world.

DUNCAN EDWARDS.

If I wanted to define him, I'd say that he's an island - but an island of freedom, generosity and pride.

GERARD HOULHER on his friend Eric Cantona.

He's so mild mannered when the volcano is not erupting inside him, and very patient with the youngsters.

ALEX FERGUSON on Eric Cantona.

Those who accept being in my shadow are the most intelligent people because they know that I make them win.

ERIC CANTONA.

He was born to play for United. Some players, with respected and established reputations, are cowed and broken by the size and expectations. Not Eric. He swaggered in, stuck his chest out, raised his head and surveyed everything as if to ask: 'I'm Cantona, how big are you? Are you big enough for me? '

ALEX FERGUSON.

I know people think I have indulged Eric. That's absolute non-sense. These are emotional people in emotional situations and we handle it as best we can. Eric is an emotional man. We try to guard him and warn him, but in certain situations his emotions can't be controlled.

ALEX FERGUSON.

My heart and my legs were made to play British football.

ERIC CANTONA.

Football and Manchester United have already let one legendary genius feel he had to walk away while he was still 27. I just hope they don't lose another one.

JIM SHELLEY, fan, on Eric Cantona.

I am very happy and very proud to get this prize tonight. I would like to say first I owe my success to Manchester United, to my manager Alex Ferguson, my coach Brian Kidd, all my team-mates, the staff, the fans. After that I would like to congratulate other people from football in England, even the players who didn't vote for me, for the pleasure they give me to play in this magnificent football, English football.

ERIC CANTONA receiving the Player of the Year Award in 1994.

It's a love story, it's a love story.

ERIC CANTONA on his relationship with United.

Eric will always do the opposite to what you expect. That's why he's such a good footballer - and why he's such a crazy or mythical character for a lot of people, but a very nice person for others who know him a little bit better. I only have words of thanks for him and respect for the great football player he is.

JORDI CRUYFF.

He stands in front of the camera like he is about to take a penalty.

ETIENNE CHATILLIER, film director, on Eric Cantona's acting debut.

I wish I could play music and talk the way I feel football.

BOBBY CHARLTON.

They know on the Continent that European football without the English is like a hot dog without mustard.

BOBBY CHARLTON.

Old Trafford is the theatre of dreams.

BOBBY CHARLTON.

Bobby Charlton almost rivals Churchill as the best known Briton of the 20th. century. Britain never had a greater sporting ambassador.

JIMMY GREAVES.

The persistent complaint I have heard made against Bobby Charlton is that he avoids the fury of the game, where the hacking and elbowing are fiercest. This is like dismissing Dickens from the world's literature greats because he neverr went to gaol for throwing bricks at politicians.

ARTHUR HOPCROFT, journalist.

Some folks tell me that we professional players are soccer slaves. Well, if this is slavery, give me a life sentence.

BOBBY CHARLTON.

Personally I don't like playing a slow game, pushing the ball around. It seems to me like kicking a man when he's down, making fun of the opposition. I suppose this is why I don't think of foreigners as being professionals in the same sense as us. They're not prepared to give everything in the same way as our fellows.

BOBBY CHARLTON.

They have made Bobby a saint at last.

GEORGE COHEN after the unveiling of a portrait of Bobby Charlton at the National Portrait Gallery.

How much further down his head will Bobby Charlton have to part his hair before he faces the fact that he is bald.

CLIVE JAMES, broadcaster and writer.

He was idolised from his twentieth year on. There has never been a more popular footballer. He was as near perfection as man and player as it is possible to be.

MATT BUSBY on Bobby Charlton

[Giggs] has sold more dummies than Mothercare.

HENRY WINTER, journalist.

Norman is from North Belfast - not the East. He's not romantic - and he's got short hair.

BOB BISHOP, United's Northern Ireland scout, comparing Norman Whiteside with George Best.

You can't be an avant-gardist in football. It's a team game.

ERIC CANTONA.

When I came in we used to be a rollercoaster outfit. We could beat anybody, but anybody could beat us.

ALEX FERGUSON.

It didn't have anything to do with the price tag or the expectation and I was never in awe of United. Admittedly the stadium was fantastic and you could play five-a-side in the restaurant. But I never felt intimidated by it all.

GARY BIRTLES.

To have a criticism of Old Trafford is almost impossible. When you're there, you're the envy of all the other players in the football league. You're playing in the best stadium in the country, you've got the biggest and best support you could hope for. How could anyone that's been there slag it off ?

LOU MACARI.

I expected the ref to award a free kick against me. But when he didn't, I wasn't going to argue.

NAT LOFTHOUSE who scored in the 1958 Cup Final after barging Harry Gregg and the ball into the net.

A goal should never have been awarded. I remember sitting seething in the bath at Wembley praying that Lofthouse wouldn't retire before I had a chance to get my own back. I'm happy to tell you that he didn't and I did.

HARRY GREGG on the same incident.

Here Harry, this one's free. We don't charge goalkeepers here.

NAT LOFTHOUSE when Harry Gregg visited his pub.

Defenders are frustrated strikers. We stand at the back watching the forwards getting all the glory.

GARY PALLISTER.

I read the game better now and I see things clearer and organise things better. So all this compensates for you when the legs go a bit.

GARY PALLISTER.

I want to deliver. In four years time I want everybody to know Poborsky.

KAREL POBORSKY.

You don't realise how good David is until you play with him. He can do so much with a ball. He has the world at his feet.

ALAN SHEARER on David Beckham.

He's one of those full-backs you think has been playing so long he must be 60.

ALEX FERGUSON on Dennis Irwin.

When I do criticise the club nowadays, it's the responsee of a supporter and not an ex-manager.

TOMMY DOCHERTY.

He is one of the few players who would have got into the pre-Munich side.

BOBBY CHARLTON on Denis Law.

It's the next best thing to playing. I hope I've got a few more years left in me yet because this is a dream job.

DARREN LIBERMANN, alias Fred the Red, the United mascot.

When I played and a goalkeeper held the ball on the goal-line he went into the back of the net.

JACK ROWLEY.

Bryan gives you the impression that your squad is bigger than it really is.

RON ATKINSON on Bryan Robson.

When the pot starts to boil it can't be stopped.

ALEX FERGUSON after United beat Juventus 3-2 in the Champion's League in 1997.

He's a man's man. You look at him and say: 'He would never rat on anyone.'

ALEX FERGUSON on Paul Scholes.

I honestly can't remember the last time I drank champagne: whether it was before or during training.

RON ATKINSON.

There are some unwritten rules the British public should know about. I'm not allowed to play any of my music because the rest of the team hate it. Every week it's the same story. I try to play Jesus and Mary Chain and end up being forced to listen to George Benson.

BRIAN McCLAIR on life on the team bus.

I told him my problem was whether to include appearance or disappearance money.

RON ATKINSON on Paul McGrath.

I don't want to change my hairstyle at all. I like it long and Alex Ferguson has said nothing about it.

KAREL POBORSKY.

I just want to play football. I want to play matches and train every day and, hopefully, win trophies.

ROY KEANE.

He likes to think he's the daddy of the team, but he's too old for that - he's the grandaddy.

LEE SHARPE on Steve Bruce.

The great tradition of the club is most obvious when we travel away, especially when we go abroad. Everyone seems to know us and the name of the club is treated with respect. We always take care to dress as smartly as possible because we are representing Manchester United.

BRIAN GREENHOFF.

When players get through into goalscoring positions, they think of too many things. I always say: 'When in doubt, blast it.'

ALEX FERGUSON.

Wearing that is like saying you go on holiday to Benidorm, you come back with a straw donkey under your arm and you wear a shell suit. The black marks are like sick that has been printed on to the fabric. Last season, it just dribbled down; this season it has been strategically placed. It's amazing. They are the biggest club and they have the worst shirt. Mr.Byrite wouldn't sell it.

WAYNE HEMINGWAY, fashion designer, on United's shirts.

You can never judge what the opposition is likely to do. Any plans should be based on the skill of your own players in adapting.

MATT BUSBY.

Given the strong squad we have here, it's better to shut up and just go where they tell you to. If there's a striker missing, I'll train to be a striker to get my place. If there's a right winger missing, I will train to get the right wing place. I don't mind.

JORDI CRUYFF.

TAKING EACH QUOTE AS IT COMES

Teddy Sheringham: there is no better name in English football. It is a name that seems to come from a different era, before the Pauls and Lees and Jasons were even thought of; a time when men were men, footballs weighed as much as suet pudding and long shorts were worn without irony.

LAURA THOMPSON, journalist.

Ole doesn't look too grown up, but he plays like a man.

HENNING BERG, then at Blackburn, on Ole Gunnar Solskjaer.

Footballers can always learn. I discovered something new in every game I played.

BILLY MEREDITH, winger in the early years of the century.

The player with the Marilyn Monroe wiggle.

DESCRIPTION of Eddie Colman.

I laid plans for coping with Best and Charlton and the other stars, but nobody warned me about this boy Aston.

THE BENEFICA manager on John Aston who was the man of the match in the 1968 European Cup Final.

I've lived like a hermit for donkeys' years, and my own social activities were practically nil.

BILL FOULKES.

Even after a skinful, I don't have a hangover and can still be up with the others.

BRYAN ROBSON.

Sharp as a needle, a brilliant little player. To be honest, I fancied him more than Duncan Edwards.

JOE MERCER on Eddie Colman.

People wondered how I would adjust. But Old Trafford folk drink tea and eat fish suppers as well you know. Why people should think it's all champagne and caviar beats me.

LOU MACARI.

The captaincy is an honour, but it's also a responsibility.

STEVE BRUCE.

I can't understand why United didn't buy his medals. They could have helped an old player when he needed it. And themselves. Bill wasn't just a member of the European Cup winners. He survived the 1958 Munich crash that cost the team that should have been the first to win that cup. That makes him special in United's history

TONY DUNNE on Bill Foulkes who was forced to sell his medals after falling on hard times.

I said before the game we'd win but your talent overwhelmed my mind.

URI GELLER, a Reading supporter, to Ryan Giggs after they were knocked out of the FA Cup.

The nearest thing to the thunder of hooves on a football pitch is a marauding Mark Hughes of Manchester United. Soft-spoken and shy away from the action, fiery and hard as a nugget of Welsh coal in the thick of it, he is the master of the spectacular strike.

THE DAILY EXPRESS.

I just wish all our games against United could end at half-time. We do well until then. Unfortunately we do have to play for the full 90 minutes.

BRIAN HORTON, then Manchester City manager.

Brave as a lion with marks to prove it.

PAT CRERAND on Kevin Moran.

TAKING EACH QUOTE AS IT COMES

With eleven Tommy Smiths you'd not only win the European Cup, you'd fancy your chances against the whole Russian Army.

MARTIN BUCHAN.

Everything is so much faster in the first team. I thought the pace would calm down after 20 minutes, but it just keeps going and going.

DAVID BECKHAM.

For the players he left behind at Manchester United, there will be one lasting memory of Garry Birtles. His weird, way-out gear... the fancy bow-ties, winged collars and spectacular suits that nobody else would wear without the courage of four bottles of wine.

STEVE COPPELL.

I may be thought odd, but when I think of Manchester United, I think of Roger Byrne, Duncan Edwards and Eddie Colman before the crash and of Harry Gregg, Bill Foulkes and Nobby Stiles afterwards. Best, Law and Crerand were replaceable somehow. They weren't the heart of the team.

BOBBY CHARLTON.

Motivation is all about firing a person's inner feelings, inspiring qualities they can't reach for themselves.

ALEX FERGUSON.

Roy doesn't need to fight to prove he's a quality player. I never thought I would be able to consider another player capable of being placed in the Edwards bracket. But Roy Keane is that player. I find him a compelling force.

HARRY GREGG.

Nihil Sine Labor. (Nothing Without Work)

THE MOTTO hanging on the wall of Alex Ferguson's office.

The players see each other from time to time. I think we are the only club who have an old players' association.

PAT CRERAND.

If Norman Whiteside had one more yard of pace he would have been one of the greatest players ever produced in British football.. He had incredible quality, an ice cold temperament. If you looked at his eyes, he just stared through opponents as if they were not there.

ALEX FERGUSON.

How could you possibly go and watch London Irish play on the same day Manchester United were playing Arsenal at Highbury ?

TONY WARD, Irish rugby international.

The club is a kind of reversal of the city's fate. Through it the lost capital city of the industrial revolution is reborn.

FINTAN O'TOOLE, journalist, on United.

There are parts of the world where Manchester United are the only English words the natives know.

EAMON DUNPHY.

If Lew Grade can make the office by six in the morning at 80 years of age. then I can make it at eight.

ALEX FERGUSON.

Footballers tend not to notice or enjoy what's around them. I remember once on a tour of Italy the coach passed the Leaning Tower of Pisa. I pointed it out, only to be told: 'Shut up and deal.'

BOBBY CHARLTON.

Unfulfilled potential is a manager's nightmare.

ALEX FERGUSON.

TAKING EACH QUOTE AS IT COMES

The circus has come to town but the lions and tigers didn't turn up.

KEVIN KEEGAN after a defeat at Old Trafford.

I was a bit wary about whether the gaffer would give me the captaincy because everyone was saying maybe I wouldn't be able to handle the responsibility with all the off-field stuff and all the worries about my temperament on the field. I wasn't expecting to be made captain, but then again I wasn't surprised either. I knew Pally [Gary Pallister] and Peter [Schmeichel] would be there or thereabouts but I was delighted when it was me.

ROY KEANE.

What a lucky guy I am to have been part of this great club success and in my first season too.

BRIAN KIDD who won a European Cup medal when he was just 17.

People tell me I should be feeling tired after playing almost non-stop for five years, but I'm not. The main thing is that I do not feel disinterested in the game.

BOBBY CHARLTON before his 500th game for United.

[Roy] Keane, who will be more of a Greta Garbo captain, like Cantona, rather than the media friendly Steve Bruce, will not alter his ways.

CHRISTOPHER DAVIES, journalist.

It was really a matter of vision. Our players said it was difficult to see their teammates at distances when they lifted their heads.

ALEX FERGUSON explaining why his players changed their strips at half-time in the match against Southampton.

It is flattering to be mentioned in the same breath as Eric Cantona.

PAUL SCHOLES.

An architect of constructive defence and almost as great in his ways as Matthews.

GEOFFREY GREEN, journalist, on Johnny Carey.

If you put the '60s attack against this United defence I know who I would back. Would Paul Parker be able to stop George Best ? Would Denis Irwin be able to stop me ?

WILLIE MORGAN in 1994.

You can't go 31 games unbeaten, aiming for the treble, by pirouetting about like a ballet dancer.

STEVE BRUCE.

I am going to make the move which will make or break Manchester United.

MATT BUSBY about to break up his first great team. The decision led to the Busby Babes.

Don't go looking for glory otherwise it will pass you by. Let it come. Work for it.

MALCOLM MUSGROVE, Frank O'Farrell's assistant.

The only one I was jealous of was George - he was better looking than me.

PAT CRERAND.

All the time the struggle was raging, the 30 Clayton chimneys smoked and gave forth their pungent odours, and the boilers behind the goal poured mists of steam over the ground.

THE GUARDIAN in 1907

Just my luck. They give me George Best's liver.

RANGERS icon Jim Baxter after a liver transplant failed.

The fact they accused Bobby Charlton of sheltering me while I 'stole ' a bracelet proves I'm innocent. Bobby has never done a dishonest thing in his life.

BOBBY MOORE who was accused of stealing a braclet in Bogota.

Look at my career. 230-odd games in the lower divisions in seven years at Gillingham. Manchester United were just people on TV to me.

STEVE BRUCE.

I don't want to sell my memorabilia because it reminds me of my great playing days. But I refuse to sign on the dole - I'm too proud for that.

BILL FOULKES who was forced to sell his medals.

A United player is a passionate mix of skill, heart and youth. Manchester United are all about flair and improvisation; a club with history and style bred on romance.

HARRY GREGG.

If I'd got that goal that Hughsie scored to equalise against Oldham in the last seconds of the FA semi, I'd have run round Wembley twice, taken my shirt off, thrown it into the crowd, then dived in after it.

RYAN GIGGS on Mark Hughes' last-minute equaliser in the semi-final of the 1994 FA Cup.

It's tough for him. But I have talked to him and he understands the position. At the moment he's a little bloody nuisance the way he keeps putting pressure on me.

ALEX FERGUSON on Paul Scholes who was not a regular in the team despite some brilliant performances.

George Best Edwardia Ltd.

THE NAME of George Best's clothes shop company.

SPEAK OF THE DEVILS

The one thing that has never changed in the history of the game is the shape of the ball.

DENIS LAW.

You have to have the same temperament as a striker. When you're playing you've got to be selfish. You've got to think, I'm sorting this out.

PETER SCHMEICHEL on goalkeepers

It was an instinct. Nothing else. You smell danger and that depth of feeling burns inside and tells you precisely the next move. I had to discard poor old Jim - the man I gave a debut to way back in 1978 - for the sake of Manchester United. There was no other decision ever in my mind.

ALEX FERGUSON after dropping goalkeeper Jim Leighton for the FA Cup Final replay against Crystal Palace in 1990.

Don't even dare ask. Just don't ask me.

JIM LEIGHTON to journalists.

I am allergic to grass ! It's why you never see me rolling around when I get injured. My problems are something I have to live with. I try not to make a big deal about it. But I know it's crazy for someone who spends half his life running around on grass.

OLE GUNNAR SOLSKJAER.

I would be faced with the choice of playing for Russia, the Ukraine or Lithuania, all of which I was eligible for. It was also possible that I might be eligible for France. Someone even told me that Jackie Charlton had made enquiries to see if I had great-grandparents with Irish blood.

ANDREI KANCHELSKIS.

Manchester United Ruined My Life.

TITLE of a book by writer, producer and City fan Colin Shindler.

You need to shoot somebody with a Tommy gun to get a penalty in a big game.

ALEX FERGUSON.

It looks as though we are going to be happy just to stay on the same page of Ceefax as Manchester United.

RON ATKINSON, then manager of Aston Villa.

His favourite television shows are the quiz programmes - especially something semi-highbrow such as *University Challenge* and he more than holds his own with the intelligentsia.

GEORGE BEST on Denis Law.

Manchester United stands for something more than any person, any player, any supporter. It is the 'soul ' of a sporting organisation which goes on season after season, making history all the time.

UNITED PROGRAMME notes from 1937.

Norman's greatest quality has always been his quality.

RON ATKINSON on Norman Whiteside.

I can meet ministers and monarchs and my children are not much impressed but when we met Alex Ferguson they realised there was some point.

TONY BLAIR, MP.

If one day, all the tacticians reached perfection, the result would be 0-0 draw and there would be nobody there to see it.

PAT CRERAND.

I don't want to be anyone's assistant but I'd go to Manchester United as kit manager

SAMMY MCILROY, Macclesfield boss and former United player.

Even the teachers had to have their affiliations. In fact, I used to sometimes wonder if they had to state their allegiance on their contracts when they came into the district.

NOBBY STILES.

In the three hours before kick-off I doubt if I ever make sense. I piddle around murdering myself.

DENIS LAW.

He's not only a good player, but he's spiteful in the nicest sense of the word.

RON ATKINSON on Norman Whiteside.

Manchester United are buzzing around the goalmouth like a lot of red blue bottles.

DAVID COLEMAN, sports commentator.

As centre halves go, Jim Holton is a bony, booted, gangling threat who patrols in defence with the soft tread of an elephant's rumba.

JULIE WELCH, journalist.

We put bells on a football so he would know where it was. We had complaints from Morris Dancers saying he was kicking them all over the place.

TOMMY DOCHERTY on Jim Holton.

I never thought I'd see the day when I'd say we needed a few more Englishmen in our squad.

ALEX FERGUSON on the UEFA restrictions on the number of foreign players allowed in European matches.

The Doc wasn't scared of the big names; he'd drop the Lou Macaris and the Stuart Pearsons and give the kids a chance.

JIMMY NICHOLL.

TAKING EACH QUOTE AS IT COMES

Old Trafford is the only stadium in the world that's absolutely buzzing with atmosphere when it's empty. It's almost like a cathedral.

TOMMY DOCHERTY.

It is a tragedy that his good points are always overshadowed by his wild inconsistencies and that part of his nature which always seems to lead him into battles with other people.

ALEX STEPNEY on Tommy Docherty.

The Doc's character was reflected in his team. It was harum-scarum, a bit unpredictable.

LOU MACARI.

I know how hard it is playing for Manchester United and I can't stress enough how much I respect the players.

BRIAN KIDD.

I absolutely loath them. What gets me about United is their ubiquity; you can't avoid them. They've even got Bobby Charlton's daughter presenting the weather.

HOWARD DAVIES, chairman of the Financial Services Association and Manchester City fan.

Manchester United are among the greatest sporting icons. We have tremendous respect for them in New Zealand, and look up to them for what they have achieved. Our aim is to try and put the All Blacks on a similar footing.

ROSS COOPER, assistant coach to the All Blacks.

It will create an atmosphere like nothing they have ever played in. The way it has been designed means that it is a great stage which every player loves playing.

BOBBY CHARLTON before the All Blacks played England at Old Trafford in 1997.

You won't find me getting involved in any of the violence that sometimes meets the Springboks in this country, but I do feel tempted sometimes to join in the peaceful sit-ins by way of demonstration, even if I feel it probably wouldn't do much good, except maybe give some of the knockers a reason to have a go at me! Fact is that the South Africans simply shouldn't be allowed here at all next summer, unless something is done about that rotten apartheid business back in their home towns.

It's pure rubbish to suggest that playing test matches at cricket will show how life should be led. Test cricket isn't a bit like real life, not life as it is today, and the many years of series between the two countries hasn't done the slightest bit of good. Meanwhile Arthur Ashe and that Indian golfer are not allowed into South Africa.

Let 'em stew in it, say I. Let 'em do without competitive international sport until the way is laid open for anybody, regardless of creed or colour, to represent his colour and get the full reward for his skill.

GEORGE BEST in 1970.

Ask all the players in the country which club they would like to join and 99% would say 'Manchester United.' The other 1% would be liars.

GORDON McQUEEN.

It is impossible to play badly in a stadium like Old Trafford.

JOHANN CRUYFF.

Joe Jordan kicks the the parts other beers cannot reach.

GRAFFITO.

It was in the character and spirit of Edwards that I saw the true revival of British football.

WALTER WINTERBOTTOM, the England manager in the late 1950s and early 1960s, on Duncan Edwards.

TAKING EACH QUOTE AS IT COMES

He was not just a player. He was a team.

JIMMY MURPHY on Duncan Edwards.

I would play football for every working hour if I could.

DUNCAN EDWARDS.

People must think I live in Gucci and Prada shops. I'm worried they'll forget I play football as well as going out with a Spice Girl.

DAVID BECKHAM.

El Beatle.

PORTUGESE NEWSPAPER'S description of George Best after his brilliant performance in United's 5-1 thrashing of Benfica in Lisbon.

El Take That

RED ISSUE, fanzine, comparing unfavourably Ryan Giggs performance against Barcelona in the 1994 European Cup with George Best's brilliant show against Benfica in the same competition in 1966.

Kid Dynamite, the Baby Giant, the Gentle Giant, Big Dunk, the Boy with the Heart of a Man.

DUNCAN EDWARDS.

These snooker players have it good. When they play a bad shot the crowd doesn't shout: 'Get off, you bum' They haven't got another ten men bolstering their confidence or ruining it.

KEVIN MORAN.

You treat every game here like a Cup Final. Otherwise you will get turned over.

VIV ANDERSON.

SPEAK OF THE DEVILS

We have the same philosophy. An honest day's work for an honest day's pay.

BRIAN KIDD on his relationship with Alex Ferguson.

Mike isn't going to get into the Old Trafford Hall of Fame like Best, Law and Charlton. He's not as celebrated as someone like Bryan Robson with his 70-odd caps. But 90 per cent of our fans will always regard him as Mr.Dependeable and that is how he gets his recognition.

ALEX FERGUSON on Mike Duxbury.

LAST WORD

I want to die at Old Trafford.

ERIC CANTONA.

My career trickled away, I suppose but, you know, all down the years I've been fulfilled by the fact that I played 17 times with the Busby Babes.

KENNY MORGANS who was injured in the Munich crash.

I'm more than happy. I've all my cartilages. I've no arthritis and I'm as busy as I've ever been.

BOBBY CHARLTON.

At the end of the day the bus goes on and we don't wait for anybody.

ALEX FERGUSON.

None of you will be around in ten years but I will. I'll still be here taking them on.

ALEX FERGUSON to journalists.

Every manager goes through life looking for one great player, praying he'll find one. I was more lucky than most. I found two - Big Duncan and George. I suppose in their own ways they both died, didn't they?

MATT BUSBY.

If I could be remembered for anything when I finished in management, it wouldn't be for all the Cups, the titles and glory. It would be for one thing - that I never deserted any one of the players I had under my control.

ALEX FERGUSON.

At the end of the day I'm just a footballer.

RYAN GIGGS.

Football has been kind to me. I wouldn't swap what's happened to me for the world..

NORMAN WHITESIDE.

I've been lucky, you know. I'd always wanted to be a footballer but I never imagined it would turn out the way it did. I've been in the right place at the right time. I could have been 20 when I played in the World Cup, not 17 and then nobody would have paid attention to my debut. I was in the right place to score that goal at Wembley.

NORMAN WHITESIDE.

The greatest time for me was always just turning up to train with the rest, and know I was a Manchester United footballer.

SHAY BRENNAN.

Now I have my memories, something that cannot be taken away from me. And I'm happy. I'm grateful to have played for United and to have got out of that aircraft alive.

ALBERT SCANLON.

When I finish here I feel sure that will be it. I can't see anything greater than this.

ALEX FERGUSON.

There is always something new to fire my enthusiasm.

ALEX FERGUSON.

They were great days. I had to keep pinching myself. My only dream was to play until I dropped.

STEVE COPPELL.

It was a lovely shirt, richer, a purer red. I'd have to pinch myself into believing it was true, this is real, you're playing in George Best's shirt. If you done that, it doesn't matter what you do after, does it?

GORDON HILL.

Cantona had his faults, he had a million faults, and was his own man. But the biggest thing he did at our club was hit home the importance of practice to attain perfection.

ALEX FERGUSON.

I don't want to go down as the gentleman of football. I would rather be remembered as a good player.

B0BBY CHARLTON.

No matter what has happened off the field since then, no matter what people think, at the end of the day they'll remember the football. They won't remember who I dated, fights and car crashes or whatever, they won't remember any of that, because it's not important. They'll remember the football.

GEORGE BEST.

I just love the drama of it all. People ask when am I going to quit. Good grief, I would miss all that purgatory.

ALEX FERGUSON.

I know there are those who would like to see me in the gutter. They'll never have that satisfaction, though.

GEORGE BEST.

I never felt that I ever let the team down or that I let myself down on the field. A lot of things were happening off the field that maybe I would have changed. I left Manchester United with a clear conscience.

GEORGE BEST.

We were not a tactical side. We just played. We should have won more than we did.

TONY DUNNE.

They can spend heavily to buy the title, but they'll have to buy forever to catch up with us.

ALEX FERGUSON.

I've always had success because I've always got people to have confidence in me, players and directors. They have always done their best for me and I have always tried to do the same for them.

MATT BUSBY.

Football in England is fundamentally different to anywhere else. It's given me a lot more than I've given it.

ERIC CANTONA.

The most important thing is the work ethic.

ALEX FERGUSON.

If my name is mentioned in football circles in the future, I just hope they say: 'He was a good professional. '

MARTIN BUCHAN.

LAST WORD

What matters above all things is that the game should be played in the right spirit, with the utmost resource of skill and courage, with fair play and no favour, with every man playing as a member of his team and the result accepted without bitterness and conceit.

MATT BUSBY.

I've been training very hard to get cliches out of my system. But it's very difficult when you come off the pitch and a reporter is looking for a quote. It's dead easy to slip into verbal shorthand. I only say: 'Football is a game of two halves' if I'm taking the piss. But the cliche that catches me out most is: 'At the end of the day.' I keep telling myself to stop saying it. I keep thinking: 'Remember Brian, at the end of the day it will be 11.59 pm.'

BRIAN McCLAIR.

I really have to pinch myself from time to time to remind myself that I really did play for Manchester United.

JOHN FITZPATRICK.

If I had my time again I would be a midfielder or a striker, where you get more of the glory.

GARY BAILEY.

I've been very lucky. I could be dead.

GEORGE BEST.

You can take your Barcelonas, you can take your Real Madrids. Man United is the only club for me.

PHIL NEVILLE.

INDEX

INDEX

INDEX

87,113,114,117,120,139,140,146.

Wilkins, Ray,5,97.
Wilkinson, Howard,71.
Willis, Peter,57.
Wilson, Harold,1.
Winter, Henry,110,126.
Winterbottom, Walter,142.
Woolridge, Joyce,5.